VOLUME 23

D0063895

FIRST and SECOND CORINTHIANS

Norman P. Madsen

ABINGDON PRESS
Nashville

1 and 2 Corinthians

Copyright © 1988 by Graded Press

This book is printed on recycled, acid-free paper.

Library of Congress Cataloging-in-Publication Data

Cokesbury basic Bible commentary.
  Basic Bible commentary / by Linda B. Hinton . . . [etal.].
    p.   cm.
  Originally published: Cokesbury basic Bible commentary. Nashville: Graded Press, © 1988.
  ISBN 0-687-02620-2 (pbk. : v. 1 : alk. paper)
  1. Bible—Commentaries. I. Hinton, Linda B. II. Title.
  [BS491.2.C65   1994]
  220.7—dc20   94-10965
                                                                                CIP

ISBN 0-687-02643-1 (v. 23, 1 and 2 Corinthians)
ISBN 0-687-02620-2 (v. 1, Genesis)
ISBN 0-687-02621-0 (v. 2, Exodus–Leviticus)
ISBN 0-687-02622-9 (v. 3, Numbers–Deuteronomy)
ISBN 0-687-02623-7 (v. 4, Joshua–Ruth)
ISBN 0-687-02624-5 (v. 5, 1–2 Samuel)
ISBN 0-687-02625-3 (v. 6, 1–2 Kings)
ISBN 0-687-02626-1 (v. 7, 1–2 Chronicles)
ISBN 0-687-02627-X (v. 8, Ezra–Esther)
ISBN 0-687-02628-8 (v. 9, Job)
ISBN 0-687-02629-6 (v. 10, Psalms)
ISBN 0-687-02630-X (v. 11, Proverbs–Song of Solomon)
ISBN 0-687-02631-8 (v. 12, Isaiah)
ISBN 0-687-02632-6 (v. 13, Jeremiah–Lamentations)
ISBN 0-687-02633-4 (v. 14, Ezekiel–Daniel)
ISBN 0-687-02634-2 (v. 15, Hosea–Jonah)
ISBN 0-687-02635-0 (v. 16, Micah–Malachi)
ISBN 0-687-02636-9 (v. 17, Matthew)
ISBN 0-687-02637-7 (v. 18, Mark)
ISBN 0-687-02638-5 (v. 19, Luke)
ISBN 0-687-02639-3 (v. 20, John)
ISBN 0-687-02640-7 (v.21, Acts)
ISBN 0-687-02642-3 (v. 22, Romans)
ISBN 0-687-02644-X (v. 24, Galatians–Ephesians)
ISBN 0-687-02645-8 (v. 25, Philippians–2 Thessalonians)
ISBN 0-687-02646-6 (v. 26, 1 Timothy–Philemon)
ISBN 0-687-02647-4 (v. 27, Hebrews)
ISBN 0-687-02648-2 (v. 28, James–Jude)
ISBN 0-687-02649-0 (v. 29, Revelation)
ISBN 0-687-02650-4 (complete set of 29 vols.)

98 99 00 01 02 03—10 9 8 7 6 5 4 3

MANUFACTURED IN THE UNITED STATES OF AMERICA

Contents

Outline of 1 and 2 Corinthians

First Corinthians

I. Beginning of the Letter (1:1-9)
  A. Address and blessing (1:1-3)
  B. General thanksgiving (1:4-9)
II. Encouragement and Instruction (1:10–6:20)
  A. Church members should be one in Christ (1:10-17)
  B. The centrality of the cross (1:18–2:5)
  C. God's wisdom made known in Christ (2:6-16)
  D. The foundation of Christian maturity (3:1–4:21)
  E. Immoral practices and life styles (5:1–6:20)
    1. Incest and excommunication (5:1-13)
    2. Refraining from lawsuits (6:1-11)
    3. Be firm in Christian faith (6:12-20)
III. Answers to Practical Questions (7:1–12:31)
  A. Questions about marriage (7:1-40)
  B. Concerns about food and dietary practices (8:1-13)
  C. Paul's apostolic responsibility (9:1–11:1)
  D. The practice of public worship (11:2–12:31)
    1. Men and women in worship (11:2-16)
    2. Celebrating the Lord's Supper (11:17-34)
    3. Comments about spiritual gifts (12:1-31)
IV. Directives Concerning Important Issues (13:1–15:58)
  A. The superiority of love (13:1-13)
  B. Speaking in tongues (14:1-40)
  C. The meaning of the resurrection of Christ (15:1-58)
V. Paul's Concluding Comments (16:1-24)
  A. Update on collections for the needy (16:1-4)
  B. Travel plans and work of helpers (16:5-18)
  C. Final greetings (16:19-24)

Second Corinthians

I. Beginning of the Letter (1:1-11)
   A. Address and general blessing (1:1-2)
   B. General thanksgiving (1:3-11)
II. Paul's Sincere Concern (1:12–3:3)
   A. Why Paul did not come to Corinth (1:12–2:4)
   B. Paul's apostolic commission (2:5–3:3)
III. The Old and New Covenants (3:4-18)
IV. Paul's Ministry by God's Mercy (4:1–7:4)
   A. Paul an ambassador of Christ (4:1–5:21)
   B. Paul's love of the Corinthians in Christ (6:1-13)
   C. The Corinthians must cling to Christ (6:14–7:4)
V. Appeals for Sincerity in Christ (7:5–9:15)
   A. Paul rejoices in news about them (7:2-16)
   B. Collection for Jerusalem believers (8:1–9:15)
VI. Paul's Authority as an Apostle (10:1–13:10)
   A. Boasting and laboring in the Lord (10:1-18)
   B. Paul is a fool for Christ (11:1–12:13)
   C. Appeal for renewal in Christ (12:14–13:10)
VII. Paul's Concluding Comments (13:11-14)
   A. A final appeal (13:11-13)
   B. A blessing of grace (13:14)

Introduction to 1 and 2 Corinthians

Paul's letters to the Christians at Corinth are fascinating. They are addressed to new believers living in a rather fast-paced city. They speak of believers' problems that have become very evident in a modern world surprisingly similar to life in the Corinth of long ago. They contain one of the most profound prose passages in the history of literature (1 Corinthians 13). They focus the believer's attention on the essentials of the Christian faith. And they explain the Christian answer to the great human dread that faces all, death and extinction (1 Corinthians 15). Before we look at the text of the letters, we must ask what is known about the city of Corinth, those to whom the letter is addressed, and the author of the letters.

The City of Corinth

Corinth was an important city because of its location. It was situated on a small portion of land that connected the mainland of Greece with the peninsula called Pelponnesus (meaning literally a *foregoing island*; see the map on page 158). This peninsula was the site of the famous Peloponnesian War between Athens and Sparta (421–404 B.C.). Also on the peninsula was Olympia, the ancient religious center of worship where the olympic games were held in honor of the Greek god Zeus. Corinth was the connecting city between this historically important island and mainland Greece. Athens was less than fifty miles to the east.

The city of Corinth was also a port city. It actually supplied access to two bodies of water. Corinth was positioned on the Mediterranean Sea and, by way of a short two-mile canal, the Aegean Sea north of Greece was accessible. As a port city, Corinth would have been very cosmopolitan, bursting with activity. Interesting people, new trends and ideas, plenty of employment opportunities, cultural activities, and athletic contests contributed to life in Corinth. As in any port city of the Roman Empire in the first century, there also would have been a certain amount of crime, licentiousness, and sexual promiscuity evident. Hence Corinth was in many respects a very "modern" city.

Historically, Corinth thrived from the tenth to the first century B.C. Because Corinth headed a league of cities (the Achaian League), Rome perceived Corinth as a threat and eventually sacked the city in 146 B.C. One hundred years later Julius Caesar brought many freed Italian slaves to the city, reconstituting its population. According to archaeological inscriptions, this Italian influence remained. Recent excavated city ruins indicate that Latin remained a formal language for the Corinthians. Yet Greek would have been the common language because of local Grecian influences and citizenry.

Apparently Corinth had a fairly strong Jewish population. At various times in Jewish history following the Babylonian Captivity of 586 B.C., Jews from Palestine emigrated throughout the Mediterranean world and beyond. Corinth would have been an attractive city for immigration because of the cosmopolitan population and the strong economy. So it is not surprising that in Corinth Paul met two Jewish converts, Aquila and Priscilla (Acts 18:1-3; 1 Corinthians 16:19), who had been exiled from Rome because of the emperor Claudius's (10 B.C.–A.D. 54) edict, probably issued about A.D. 49. Also, Jewish synagogues have been excavated by archaeologists, indicating a strong and active Jewish population.

Paul the Evangelist

Attempting to establish the movements and activities of Paul the apostle have proven difficult. When and where he traveled and wrote his letters is not always clear. Portions of the Acts of the Apostles and Galatians, along with a few biographical notations from Paul's other letters, are the only pieces of the puzzle available. Paul's primary concern was to tell the good news of Christ. His own welfare and activity were secondary to this concern. Hence we have little evidence for reconstructing his life and activities. It is not clear when he was born, when he died, whether he saw or even heard Jesus, and so forth. (See the chronological table of Paul's life on page 17.)

However, there is one clear piece of evidence that helps us date Paul's activities with the Corinth Christians. The evidence is the dates of the Roman proconsul or tribunal in Corinth, Gallio. According to the account of Paul's activities in Acts (18:1-18), Paul's preaching in the Jewish synagogue brought him into serious conflict with the local Jews. Paul was told in a vision to stay in Corinth despite the tension, and he stayed *a year and six months* (Acts 18:11). The Jews finally brought a lawsuit against Paul (Acts 18:12-17) and Paul was brought before the local Roman tribunal, Gallio.

According to an inscription found at an archaeological excavation in Delphi, Gallio was proconsul in either 51–52 or 52–53. The first date fits better into Gallio's activities. Assuming Paul was in Corinth for almost two years, and considering Gallio's dates as proconsul, Paul must have founded the church in Corinth between the years A.D. 51 to 53 (see also 1 Corinthians 3:5-15). This mission work was done during the latter part of Paul's second missionary journey (A.D. 50–53; see Acts 15:36-41).

The Christian community was comprised of numerous

house churches. These cells of Christians included both Gentiles (Acts 18:6) and Jews (1 Corinthians 1:22-24). Sometimes Paul refers to these individual cells in his writings (see, for example, 1 Corinthians 1:16; 16:19). On other occasions, Paul seems to address all the cell groups as the church, suggesting that on occasion all got together—perhaps to hear one of Paul's letters (Romans 16:23; 1 Corinthians 14:23). The number of Christians in Corinth, the number of house churches, and the average number in a house church are almost impossible to estimate. The number of Christian converts was not great. Hence, we could estimate that in a city the size of Corinth (which probably had a population of about 100,000), there were perhaps only about fifty to one hundred converts when Paul wrote his letters. If we very roughly estimate ten persons to a house church, Paul was writing to about five to ten house churches.

While resident in Corinth, Paul supported himself by working at his learned trade of tentmaking (Acts 18:1-3). This trade was also referred to as "working with leather" because portable shelters used by shepherds, soldiers, and nomadic peoples were often fashioned from animal skins. It is probable that Paul worked in one of the small shops at the busy and popular bazaar or marketplace in Corinth.

Pursuing his trade, Paul would have come into contact with people from many different trades and with common laborers from the Corinth work force. As a result, many of Paul's converts probably came from a lower socio-economic background. Later Paul writes to the Corinth Christians referring to the *low and despised in the world* (1 Corinthians 1:28) and those who are slaves or free (1 Corinthians 7:21; 12:13). But the church also would have had at least a handful of educated and wealthier individuals (Acts 18:8; Romans 16:23; 1 Corinthians 1:14—Paul probably wrote his letter to the Christians in Rome from Corinth). These wealthier folk would have perhaps supplied the villas and homes where house churches met for worship.

The Social Setting

The first Corinthian house churches experienced some social tensions. First, there were tensions between Jews and Gentiles. Many of the Jews felt that their religious heritage was important for any who believed Jesus of Nazareth was the expected messiah. Hence they had to become Jews before they could become Christians! (See Paul's letter to the Galatians.) But Paul merely emphasizes that Christ is everything and Jewish practices are no longer valid for a right relationship with God.

There were also tensions between the social classes. The Christian faith brought together people from various backgrounds and social classes. It was a Roman custom to rank people at communal meals according to social standing in the community. Thus when house churches in Corinth held communal meals, Roman customs intensified the setting. It is not surprising then to find Paul addressing such problems with characteristic keenness and intensity (read 1 Corinthians 11:17-34 with this tension in mind).

There were also tensions over leadership. Paul says at the beginning of his first letter, . . . *Each of you says, "I belong* [NRSV; NIV= *follow*] *to Paul," or "I belong to Apollos," or "I belong to Cephas"* [Peter], *or "I belong to Christ." Has Christ been divided?* (1 Corinthians 1:12-13; for Apollos's visit, see Acts 18:27–19:1; 1 Corinthians 3:4-9; 4:6). Paul's question is not surprising considering the situation in Corinth. With many house churches that rarely would have gathered in one place, competition and jostling for superiority would have been a natural development—as is sometimes evident in churches today!

Finally, there were apparently tensions with pagan religious groups in the city. Because the Corinthians seem to have attributed great importance to knowledge or wisdom (Greek *gnosis*), many scholars have argued that Gnosticism (see the Glossary) influenced the believers of Corinth (1 Corinthians 1:5, 20-22; 3:18-19; 8:1). Although the source of this influence is not at all clear, there does appear to be a tension between a pagan-type knowledge and Christian wisdom. Perhaps a clearer indication of a Gnostic social tension between Christian believers and pagan religions was a question Paul was asked to address: Should believers eat foods dedicated to the gods of pagan religions (1 Corinthians 8:1-13)?

The Letters of Paul

The Corinthians epistles offer us at least two advantages: They are an excellent example of the way in which Paul wrote letters, and they contain what he considered to be the essence of the Christian faith.

Paul's style of writing reflects the Roman habits of his day. His letters normally contain an opening statement of greeting identifying sender and addressee (1 Corinthians 1:1-3). Then follows a general thanksgiving (1 Corinthians 1:4-9). Following these customary rituals, a message is presented that functions as the body of the letter (1 Corinthians 1:10-15:58). Finally an ending or farewell is offered, including comments about activities and intentions of Paul and his companions (1 Corinthians 16:1-24).

For the most part, Paul's letters are always courteous and considerate. They attempt to address the down-to-earth concrete situations and problems with which the various Christian communities of the Mediterranean world struggled. But at times Paul does become less than gentle with his new converts. He refers to the Galatians as being *foolish* and *bewitched* (Galatians 3:1; his emotion is also expressed in Galatians 4:19). He affectionately refers to the Christians at Thessalonica as children in need of nursing (1 Thessalonians 2:7-8; see also 3:7-8). And to the Corinthians he speaks of his *hardship* and *anxiety for all the churches* that have made him *indignant* about their fall from the true gospel (2 Corinthians 11:21-29).

What is Paul's understanding of the Christian faith? Because Paul is dealing with complexities of social classes, differing religious backgrounds (Jews and Gentiles), and divided cell groups, he states his understanding of the essential Christian message in the Corinthian epistles.

First of all, Paul emphasizes the resurrection of Christ. Because of Paul's experience on the Damascus road (Acts 9:1-22), he knows Christ is alive. His summary of the gospel to the Christians at the city of Corinth emphasizes that Christ was *raised on the third day* and appeared to many, *and appeared also to me* (1 Corinthians 15:3-8). Because Christ is alive, those who are in Christ are a *new creation* (2 Corinthians 5:17). The theme of Christ's resurreciton emanates from every thought and idea Paul struggles to communicate—it leaps from every line of his letters. It is the driving force behind his enthusiasm, his excitement, and his energetic communication of the Christian faith.

Second, Paul emphasizes the work of the Holy Spirit. The Spirit of God is the Spirit of the resurrected and living Christ. Paul deeply and profoundly experiences the Spirit of the living Christ in all his missionary activity following his experience on the Damascus road. He understands the Spirit as the practical experience of Christ working in all of the Christian life. There is no Christian activity without the Spirit (1 Corinthians 1:27-30). This same Spirit not only works within all Christian activity, but the Spirit also gives gifts to individuals for the upbuilding of the community.

For Paul, these two Christian truths cannot be disputed. The living Christ and the work of the Spirit are two necessities of the Christian's faith that will even rescue and reconstitute the fussing Corinthian believers.

These two experiential truths are emphasized again and again throughout the Corinthian correspondence. In fact, all the other issues that Paul addresses in his letters to Corinth assume these two intensely practical beliefs.

The Number of Corinthian Letters

How many letters did Paul write to the Corinthians? We have two clear letters in our New Testament, but were there other letters? The question has been raised by Paul's own statements. He refers to his previous letter in the 1 Corinthians epistle (1 Corinthians 5:9-11), which would suggest that 1 Corinthians is not his first letter. Because of the immorality theme of this previous letter (1 Corinthians 5:9), at least a portion of it could be identified with the same theme found in a section of 2 Corinthians (6:14-7:1). If this previous letter is contained in 2 Corinthians, then it would follow that 2 Corinthians is comprised of several communications from Paul to the Corinthian churches. Estimates among scholars as to the number of Paul's epistles that possibly have been combined to form 2 Corinthians range from two letters to seven letters.

If shorter communications of Paul have been blended into this letter, on the one hand they probably would have been copied together in order to make them available for all the cell house churches. On the other hand, the more communications that are identified, the more difficult is the editing process. That is to say, someone close to Paul would have sought to blend the writings in a manner that met the needs of the believers in Corinth during the latter half of the first century A.D. and that accurately communicated Paul's teachings. (It does appear that three different writings of Paul can be identified in 2 Corinthians: chapters 1–9, the excerpt in 6:14–7:4, and chapters 10–13.) Over a period of time, these letters would have been viewed as one document. But regardless of how many letters are combined in 2 Corinthians, we will understand the letter as teachings, explanations, and directives of Paul to those at Corinth.

And regardless of how many letters are identified in both 1 and 2 Corinthians, we have before us two outstanding New Testament books attributed to Paul. Throughout the writings, he struggles with every ounce of energy to keep the diverse Corinthian believers on course with regard to the Christian faith.

The Time and Occasion for These Letters

Paul wrote 1 Corinthians from the city of Ephesus (1 Corinthians 16:8). The year was A.D. 54 or 55. Although it had not been long since his departure, Paul received a report from Chloe's people (1 Corinthians 1:11) telling of tensions, rivalries, and general confusion over lifestyles and beliefs. Paul was asked to help sort out the problems. His response was the New Testament letter entitled 1 Corinthians.

Second Corinthians is far more difficult to date. If there is more than one letter from Paul contained in 2 Corinthians, then different occasions and circumstances would have to be identified. However, even if there is more than one letter contained in 2 Corinthians (many scholars argue that chapters 1–9 and 10–13 are two separate letters), Paul was writing not long after his 1 Corinthians epistle. Probably about one year later, that is, A.D. 55 or 56, Paul met with Titus in Macedonia and was greatly encouraged because of what he heard about the believers at Corinth (2 Corinthians 7:5-9). This news may have encouraged Paul to dash off a letter telling of his care for the Corinthian believers (chapters 1–9). It was perhaps a little later that Paul received some disturbing news and wrote again, attacking the *false apostles* (2 Corinthians 11:13).

Paul's Opponents at Corinth

Finally, a word about Paul's opponents in Corinth. In the 1 Corinthians letter, Paul addresses a host of problems. To explain the many problems of sexual relationships (1 Corinthians 4:1-13), marriage (7:1-16), spiritual wisdom (2:6-16), death (chapter 15), and so forth to one particular group of people—or even to one house church—seems improbable. Paul's first letter more accurately reflects various tensions, disagreements, and opinions from any number of groups (including Gnostic groups) that made the young house churches on occasion creak and groan.

However, Paul does refer specifically to some opponents in his second letter (2 Corinthians 10–13). He refers to these persons with great sarcasm, calling them *super-apostles* (2 Corinthians 11:5; 12:11). They apparently claimed that Paul did not give the Corinthians proper leadership and authority (2 Corinthians 10:10). Furthermore, Paul refused to accept financial and material support from the Corinthians (2 Corinthians 11:7-12 and 12:13-15), and now Paul took a collection for the poor (2 Corinthians 12:16-18). Finally, there was a claim about unusual spiritual gifts and experiences (1 Corinthians 12:1-11). Although Paul was probably referring to specific individuals when he called them *super-apostles,* the problems Paul addressed are too varied to identify a particular group or single resistance to Paul's ministry. Unless some new or unexpected information surfaces, Paul's opponents in Corinth will remain lost to antiquity.

Main Events in the Life of Paul

An overview of Paul's life will help identify the years of relationship and fellowship he enjoyed with the Corinthians. Because Paul was not interested in telling churches about his own importance and career, very little information is available about his life. The primary sources are 2 Corinthians 11:16-33; Galatians 2:1-10; and scattered bits from his other letters. The secondary source is the book of Acts, written by the author of Luke's Gospel. From these sources, we can attempt to reconstruct Paul's years in the following manner. (It is worth consulting various biblical commentaries for other date estimates.)

1 AND 2 CORINTHIANS

Main Events of Paul's Life

Birth of Paul	A.D. 10
Death of Christ	30
Conversion of Paul	31–32
Years in Arabia (Galatians 1:17)	32–34
Damascus and Jerusalem	34–35
Hidden years in Tarsus	35–46
Barnabas brings Paul to Antioch	46–47
Second Jerusalem visit (Acts 15)	47
First missionary journey	47–48
Third Jerusalem visit	49
Second missionary journey	50–53
Paul in residence at Corinth (Acts 18:11)	51–53
Third missionary journey	53–57
Letter of Paul to the Corinthians now lost (1 Corinthians 5:9-11)	53–54
Corinth's letter to Paul (1 Corinthians 7:1; 8:1)	53–54
Report from Chloe's people (1 Corinthians 1:11-12)	53–54
Second Corinthian letter—from Ephesus (First Corinthians)	54–55
Paul briefly visits Corinth (2 Corinthians 2:1)	54–55
Third letter to Corinth (2 Corinthians 10–13)	54–55
Titus meets Paul in Macedonia; report on Corinth (2 Corinthians 2:5-11; 7:6-13)	55–56
Fourth Letter to Corinth (2 Corinthians 1–9)	55–56
Paul's final visit (1 Corinthians 16:1-9; Romans 15:25-27)	56
Jerusalem arrest (Acts 21:27–22:29)	56–57
Trials, journey to Rome, house arrest in Rome (Acts 23:30–28:31)	57–62
Martyrdom in Rome under Nero	62–64

Although these dates are approximate, they suggest two things. First of all, Paul had very little time with the Corinthian believers. His relationship with them, based on visits and letters, lasted only about five years (this was longer, however, than Paul spent with most of his fledgling churches). It is not surprising that the Corinthians would have looked back on Paul's teachings and visits with great fondness in the decades to come. It also would have been natural for them to treasure his letters, holding them in great esteem. This great respect for Paul's letters eventually influenced the universal church to include Paul's writings in the New Testament Scriptures.

Second, Paul's correspondence always addresses and responds to real life situations. On occasion Paul's letters may sound profound and theological—they did to some Corinthians (2 Corinthians 10:10). But this is because Paul attempts to encourage believers to live in thankful response to God's grace in Christ from their particular station in life. This was certainly the situation throughout his sometimes stormy relationship with the believers at Corinth. In this sense, the Corinthian epistles are a wonderful example of ministry for laity and pastors.

The Importance of These Epistles

In Paul's day, Corinth must have been an exciting and very modern place. The problems and difficulties of the first Christians in that fast-paced city of Corinth remain very real issues today. Questions of wisdom, Christian knowledge, lifestyles, death, love, marriage, worship, suffering, and so forth remain very serious issues for believers of all ages. Because Paul boldly addresses these Christian concerns, the Corinthians correspondence is a major help in working through these ever-present Christian issues. Here, perhaps more than anywhere else, Paul achieves a profound balance between doctrinal statement and practical Christian living.

1 Corinthians 1:1-9

Introduction to These Verses

As noted in the Introduction, Paul's letters generally follow the Roman custom of letter writing. Paul begins with a courteous greeting, identifying himself and the recipients of his letter. In modern terminology, these opening lines of Paul act as a type of letterhead.

This opening greeting also sets the stage for what is about to happen. As is still the custom in many cultures, it is polite to talk generally as a form of greeting before serious conversation occurs. Paul knows his addressees very well. Yet he does not rush immediatley into issues he has on his mind. He is careful to set the stage respectfully and correctly.

The Address and the Blessing (1:1-3)

Paul begins by identifying himself and his authority. Indeed, the Corinthians would have known his name. But he does not simply say, "My name is Paul, your friend." He carefully qualifies why they should know and respect his name. Their respect has nothing to do with any qualities or abilities Paul has. In fact, throughout the letters, Paul continually diminishes his own person and indicates that God is strong because of his (Paul's) many weaknesses (1:27; 2:1-4; 2 Corinthians 11:30).

Why should Paul be respected? It is all God's doing, and it is spelled out in four themes. The first theme is Paul's calling. Paul was called by God. Paul had nothing to do with his calling. He did not earn God's favor. He had no special talents that God desired. He was simply called, chosen by God, as Israel was chosen. As God called Isaiah (Isaiah 6:1-8), Jeremiah (Jeremiah 1:1-10), and Moses (Exodus 3:1-12), and as God calls individuals throughout history, so God called Paul to a special work. And Paul wants the Corinthians to be well aware that he comes to them only because God has determined that he should be about God's work. Under no other circumstances can Paul wish to address them.

Paul has always had a deep and profound sense of his being called by God. This understanding of calling is basic to his sense of ministry. Paul's perception of his calling seems to have been magnified by his previous work—that of destroying the followers of Jesus (Acts 9:1-9; Galatians 1:13-17). When he was called by the living Jesus, he, more than most, must have realized that his calling could only be the work of God.

The second theme he mentions in the opening line is *the will of God.* Paul's radical conversion and assignment from God are a testimony to God's ever-present work in the midst of humanity. God's will is being worked out and brought to completion. Often signs and indications of God's will may not seem evident and clear. But Paul is a witness that God is at work.

Third, Paul is called to be an *apostle.* The word *apostle* carries a double meaning, based upon its Greek and Hebrew usage. The Greek understanding emphasizes the authority one carries in going out to teach; the Hebrew understanding emphasizes the message one speaks. Certainly, following the Greek use of the term, Paul is often confronted with questions of his authority (see 2 Corinthians 10–13; Galatians 1:11-24), probably because he is not one of the original disciples of Jesus. In the Hebrew sense, Paul's message is one of good news that tells of the resurrected Christ. Thus Paul is assuring the

1 AND 2 CORINTHIANS

Corinthians of both his authority and the validity of his message.

Fourth, Paul points out that he is *of Christ Jesus.* Jesus is the "christened one," the Christ, who lives. Paul's coming to the Corinthian believers is not dependent upon a past historic event that is now over and done with. Christ lives! And because he lives, Paul comes to the Corinthians with a living authority, a dynamic presence—which is Christ's and not Paul's.

Paul establishes from the beginning his true identity. He then refers to Sosthenes as a *brother,* a brother in Christ (possibly the Sosthenes of Acts 18:17). Because they are together sons of the Father through Christ, they are true brothers—spiritual brothers. But Paul is especially *called to be an apostle of Christ Jesus by the will of God.*

Then Paul clarifies to whom he writes. He identifies his audience as majestically as he has identified himself. First he asserts that the Christians in Corinth are the *church of God.* The Greek word for church, *ecclesia,* means assembly. One assembly or house church is the church universal. What applies to the individual assembly applies to the whole church. Why? As Paul understands his apostleship, so he understands the church. Both come from God. Paul is called *by the will of God* and the church is *the church of God* because God called it into existence.

Second, the Christians at Corinth are *sanctified in Christ Jesus.* They are set apart, made holy by God's grace. They have been sanctified; they have already been put right with God through the work of Christ Jesus. Paul seems to get their attention by telling them in the midst of their squabbles that they are already justified and therefore sanctified in a new and everlasting covenant.

Third, Paul explains that they are *called to be saints* (NRSV; NIV= *holy*). Previously Paul has spoken of his special calling as an apostle. Here Paul speaks of every believer's calling. Everyone is called to be a "saint" by living in thankful response for what Christ has done. To be a saint is to live thankfully. Believers do not earn sainthood. Everything has been completed by Christ. Nor is sainthood merited. Rather, by his life, death, and resurrection/ascension, Christ has sanctified humanity to God. Now all those in every place who call on Christ are the holy ones, the saints, the justified who have accepted the gift of new life and are living as saints—living in thankful response to God through Christ. These are the true saints of the church, a universal and final extension of God's people (Exodus 19:6).

Fourth, Christ is their one Lord. This not only makes all the house churches of Corinth one in Christ; but it also unites Paul and the believers of Corinth. In the power of Christ, all believers come together under one great authority. Here Paul prepares his readers for the theme of unity and oneness that he is about to stress (1 Corinthians 1:10), a theme that was a key issue for the believers in Corinth.

Then Paul writes an expression of good will—Christian good will (see Romans 1:7). He does not simply greet the Corinthians or wish them the Jewish peace; he prays for them. He offers an open prayer, emphasizing God's *grace* and *peace*. God's grace is God's action toward humanity and for humanity (1 Corinthians 15:10; 2 Corinthians 8:9). Peace is the result of God's grace, the result of a correct, right, and healthy relationship between God and humanity (Romans 5:1; 1 Corinthians 7:15).

General Thanksgiving (1:4-9)

Paul continues with an extended thanksgiving. He has already identified very carefully the participants in this conversation. The simple reason they can dialogue together is God. Their *Father* has brought them together in *the Lord Jesus Christ* (verse 3). but being together in Christ does not erase contentions, problems, lifestyle questions, and so forth. Rather, their togetherness in

Christ accentuates unnecessary frictions. These need to be eliminated, and this Paul will address in the body of the letter.

Paul begins by giving thanks to God, not to the Corinthians. He has already clearly stated that the believers in Corinth are called, sanctified, and traveling saints with Paul because God's grace was acted out in Christ. So Paul gives thanks to God because God established the Corinthian believers. Paul had spent time with the Corinthians (see the Introduction), preaching, teaching, and pointing them to Christ. Now, months later, he still takes no credit for their life of faith. The *grace of God* is the essence of their spiritual beauty. This richness comes in every way, totally, but especially in two particular ways that seem to have appeal for the churches at Corinth. The believers are enriched in *speech and knowledge.* Later in this letter Paul will deal with the gift of speech, including speaking in tongues (chapters 12 and 14), and the gift of wisdom (chapter 2). Here Paul emphasizes that these special gifts are clear examples of the Corinthian believers' wealth from God's grace through Christ. God is truly with them, and for this Paul gives God thanks.

The richness of God's grace has come through *testimony* (verse 6). Paul's initial testimony to Christ or his preaching did not fall on deaf ears. The manner in which Paul uses the term *testimony* suggests that the living Christ speaks through human preaching and testimony (see Romans 10:14, 17). So it was Christ who spoke to them through Paul's preaching. The confirmation of which Paul speaks is not convicing proof of his preaching, but of Christ's speaking and presence with them. Their experience confirms Christ.

Paul assures them that they are not lacking in *any spiritual gift* (verse 7). All the diverse gifts given to the many members of the house churches in Corinth together comprise all God's spiritual gifts and God's full blessings (Romans 8:32). Each person contributes and each has been given an adequate measure for the community (Romans 12:6; 1 Corinthians 12:4-7). These gifts are the accoutrements, the equipment, the believer's sustenance for waiting, for keeping guard, for watching for Christ's return.

Who will sustain the Corinthian believers? Christ will keep them to the end. The living Christ will be faithful to them until *the day of our Lord* (or *the day of the* LORD, Amos 5:18). They may struggle in their faith—and Paul is about to address their difficulties—but Christ will remain faithful and sure. Because he has already lived a life of perfect response, worship, and obedience to the Father for humanity, Christ's righteousness will keep them *blameless* to the end of time and throughout eternity. This is the Christian joy!

§ § § § § § §

The Message of 1 Corinthians 1:1-9

Using the normal format of letter writing for his age, Paul clarifies the three parties in his letter. God is the main actor, Paul is the called apostle, and the Corinthians are those called to faith. Everything is initiated by God and sustained by God through Christ. Thus the assurance of the Corinthians is that God will not leave them alone. Although they may have questions and they may be experiencing difficulties in the daily living out of their faith, strength and certainty come from God through the finished work of Christ.

From the beginning, Paul is enthusiastic and full of confidence. But his confidence is not in his own ability to solve the problems in Corinth. Paul's confidence is in God's plan through Christ to bring the Corinthian believers to the end of their spiritual journey—*blameless on the day of our Lord Jesus Christ.*

§ § § § § § §

PART TWO 1 Corinthians 1:10–2:5

Introduction to These Verses

The Corinthians must have been a very sensitive and explosive group. To this point in the letter Paul has been delicate and quite formal. He has approached the situation cautiously but positively. Now he begins to penetrate more severely. But he does so by continually focusing on Christ. He is seeking to help the Corinthian believers bring everything—all their problems, difficulties, tensions, misunderstandings—to Christ. Paul can help them only if they see everything in the light of Christ. He has already hinted at a problem in his formal introduction: Individual spiritual gifts are meant to benefit the total community (verse 7). Paul now begins to speak more directly.

Church Members Are One in Christ (1:10-17)

Paul begins by appealing to or begging the brethren. He wants them to agree and be united in mind and judgment. That is a humanly impossible wish and request! But Paul does not beg in the name of himself or some other human authority. He begs in the name of *our Lord Jesus Christ.* Agreement, unity, and judgment can only be achieved when believers speak, act, think, and will from Christ. They must struggle to relate to their brothers and sisters out of their relationship with Christ, which alone destroys cliques, party divisions, and factions. Paul then refers to a report from Chloe (verse

25

11). This is the first woman Paul mentions in all his letters; but unfortunately there is no other information about her. It is not even clear from this passage whether she was a Christian. But some of her workers were believers, and as they traveled between Ephesus and Corinth they brought news to Paul about *quarreling.*

The quarreling took the form of various parties or factions (verse 12). Because there was no central sanctuary for Christians, the house churches would have been prone to identify with favorite missionary leaders. Paul, Apollos, and Cephas are mentioned as favorites. Paul's reference to Christ seems to be a corrective statement to the factionalism created by favorite missionaries (thus his question in verse 13). He is suggesting that there are some who correctly say that they belong to Christ.

There has been much speculation about these favorite sons. Various problems apparent in the Corinthian churches, such as dietary questions (1 Corinthians 8:11-13), the importance of wisdom (2:1), questions about marriage (7:1-40), and others have been related to factional groups headed (perhaps unknowingly) by these missionary leaders. But because there is no certainty in identifying party beliefs, it is better for our purposes to maintain Paul's basic argument, that Christ is the only source for their unity.

Paul asks the seemingly ridiculous question, *Is Christ divided?* (NIV, verse 13). Because in a very real sense the church is Christ (12:12), to divide the church is to divide Christ. Their silly divisions are made even more bizarre in the light of two important early church beliefs, crucifixion and baptism. Paul holds these two truths together because they are Christ's work. Because he was crucified, and died for sin, believers are baptized into him (Acts 2:38; 8:16). Now Christ owns them (1 Corinthians 3:23), not Paul or Apollos or Cephas.

Paul did not baptize many while in Corinth (verses

14-16). This is somewhat surprising (although Paul explains why in verse 17). The handful that he did baptize are mentioned directly. Crispus was probably the synogogue leader (Acts 18:8) and Gaius was most likely the one who hosted Paul and had a church meeting in his house (Romans 16:23). Paul's argument is that because he has baptized so few, none can claim authority in Paul's name (verse 15). Then Paul adds a footnote, recalling that he had baptized Stephanus and his household (family and possibly slaves; see 1 Corinthians 16:15-18). Probably Paul baptized only the first converts of a region (16:15).

Then Paul gives the reason for his reluctance to baptize. His calling by Christ is to proclaim the gospel, not to baptize. Paul's understanding of his call to *preach* (NIV; NRSV= *proclaim*) is closer to what we call *teaching* today. This letter is a good example of Paul's preaching/teaching. Paul is an evangelist, but one who offers depth and substance to the message of Christianity. His calling is to educate Gentiles and Jews about the truth of God in Christ. His preaching is more than a mere emotional appeal. When an emotional evangelistic appeal is made, Paul explains here, the power and truth of Christ's cross is emptied and made frivolous.

Perhaps the Corinthian believers, because of their interest in spiritual gifts, were fond of eloquent speech. Paul turns them back to the Christ and the cross. Even if they speak in tongues, they can find no direction, except in the power of the cross.

The Centrality of the Cross (1:18–2:5)

Now Paul turns his attention to the cross of Christ. The message that God's son died on a cross is *foolishness* (verse 18). Persons outside the Christian faith, who do not believe, are in the process of *perishing*, falling farther and farther away from God. In contrast, those who believe are being saved. In neither case does Paul refer to an individual's status that is complete and definite. In each case there is ongoing falling away and being saved. For Paul, the mere presence of the living Christ means that the true believer must live daily in thankful response to God.

Quoting the Old Testament prophet Isaiah (29:14), Paul confirms what he has just said in verse 19. Eloquence and wise sayings and wisdom are human distractions from the gospel. The gospel is based solely in action, God's action through Christ on the cross. Paul is implying that true *wisdom* (and cleverness) are really far more than human speech. Human wisdom and cleverness are merely incomplete thought patterns and ways of thinking. But Paul's argument is that all true thinking and real wisdom come from God's work in Christ or begin with Christ. Other ways of human thinking are sheer folly.

Now he asks for these humanly wise persons to be identified. Name some individuals whose wisdom has withstood the test of time. Name one person who has penetrated the very truth of the universe—the very being of God. In the end, human efforts to find and know God are futile. Human efforts are incomplete. In the end God makes human efforts *foolish* by penetrating through all the lofty thoughts of human wisdom to the very existence of humanity. God was in Christ *reconciling the world to himself* (2 Corinthians 5:19; see also Colossians 1:19-20). Paul understood this truth not as merely a good idea, but as the true act of God.

Paul now gives a further commentary of this profound truth (verse 21). Because God is in control of the universe, Paul explains that God's self-revelation is not explainable by human wisdom. Believers are not first sophisticated and all-wise in order to know Christ. Rather, God chose another way, a simpler way, a more profound way. By sending a Son, God sent a message to humanity, to heal things. The message is that God loves humanity. This is the foolishness of Paul's preaching: that God *so loved the world that he gave his only Son* (John 3:16). This has nothing to do with humanity or human wisdom, but it has everything to do with God. Thus Paul preaches *to save those who believe* (verse 21).

Paul now pushes the contrast between wordly wisdom and God's truth a little farther. The Jews want a *sign*. They have seen God act in the past on their behalf. In order to confirm God's further action, they seek human confirmation in the form of a sign (Matthew 12:38-39; 16:1-4; Mark 8:11; Luke 11:29). The Greeks have always trusted in wisdom (hence their philosophical schools). Human confirmation comes to them through great philosophical thoughts and ideas. Both Jews and Greeks want to see, humanly speaking, in order to confirm God's truth. Before they trust God they want to trust themselves.

Paul bases God's truth in preaching. Christ was crucified. God acted in Christ and healed the breech between God and humanity. Believers do not need great signs or profound ideas; they merely need to hear the message. In hearing the message, the living Christ speaks. Proof and assurance come only from God—God's action and speech. The need for human confirmation recedes in the face of God's action and speech. But for those who refuse to let go of their demand for signs and wisdom, for those who hold onto and hold out for their requirements, the gospel becomes a stumbling block.

However, there are those who hear the gospel (verse 24). When persons let go of their own demands and human requirements, they are in fact blessed with the very thing they give up. For those who believe, Christ becomes the sign of God's true love for humanity; and Christ becomes the beautiful and all-inclusive wisdom of God. So the very things the believer forfeits return one hundredfold and more. Now the believer does not rely upon human power and human wisdom, but upon God's power and God's wisdom. Paul's understanding of those who hear the gospel is nothing less than a deep analysis of Christian conversion.

Then Paul states in lofty terms the great difference between God and humanity (verse 25). God is not humanity and humanity is not God. Paul is making it quite clear that the gulf between God and humanity is impassable from the human side. Only God can breech the gulf. This is why the *God's foolishness is wiser* than the greatest wisdom of humanity, and *God's weakness* is stronger than the greatest strength of humanity.

Now attention is directed to the Corinthian believers. After first emphasizing how God works powerfully and wisely through Christ, Paul exemplifies what he is saying by drawing attention to the Corinthians' own preconversion status. How had God called them? They were not attracted by great signs, lofty ideas, or powerful thoughts. Simply put, most of them did not have great worldly wisdom. Most were simply people without power, wealth, or leadership roles in the Corinthian society.

Paul's analogy is interesting (verses 26-29): Just as God's wisdom seems foolish to the world, so God's choosing of the simple Corinthians seems foolish to human wisdom. Paul's emphasis indicates that there were problems in the Corinthian churches over the relationship between God's action and human wisdom. There must have been individuals who emphasized that human wisdom was the pathway to the gospel (3:21). Perhaps this is the controvery behind the factionalism mentioned earlier (1:12).

But God has a purpose in all this. When the *low and despised* receive and live the truth of God, the true nature of the high-status values of this world is fully exposed. These values are shown to be what they really are—the inventions of persons who have lost their way. God will eventually bring to naught—or will in *the day of our Lord* (verse 8) bring to nothing—the values of this world. Thus no person can boast before God or expect to be given special status because of some human ability or talent.

Now Paul puts a conclusion to his thoughts. The first part of this conclusion (verse 30) is quite difficult to render in translation. On the one hand, Paul is arguing and following what he has already said to the Corinthians, that God is the power of life in Christ Jesus. With no human help, God brings persons to Christ.

On the other hand, Christ's work is that of the Father. Christ puts humanity in right relationship with God. Paul explains that this is accomplished in four ways. First of all, Christ is our wisdom. In Christ a person comes to know God and God's will for the universe. Second, Christ is the believer's righteousness before God. Humanity is not put right by works, but only by the grace of God in Christ. Third, Christ is the believer's sanctification. Humanity is made holy, or set apart, for fellowship with God by Christ's work. Fourth, Christ is the believer's redemption. Somehow, the world, or creation, was broken loose from the Creator. In Christ the world, humanity in particular, is redeemed, united, and established in peace for eternity.

Paul then quotes the prophet Jeremiah (verse 31). Based on the fourfold work of Christ noted above, the Corinthian believer can only boast in the Lord. Perhaps having used this text for a sermon (Jeremiah 9:23-24), Paul concludes that the work of Christ is from God, by God, and for God.

Paul concludes this section with a simple testimony (2:1-5). He has used the Corinthian believers as an example of God's divine foolishness (1:26-29); now he uses himself. He does not come to them with great wisdom or eloquence. Nor does he rely upon their great wisdom. His testimony to God is very simple: God sent the Son to put us right with God.

The word *testimony* is changed to *mystery* in some early

manuscripts. Whether intended or accidental, this word change gives us a further commentary on the passage. Paul proclaims the mystery or testimony of God, in that God chooses to have fellowship with humanity. God loves humanity. Why God chooses to have fellowship with humanity and how this is accomplished in Christ is a mystery. Paul can only testify to this truth.

Paul's testimony was nothing but the mystery of God's grace and love (2:2). Paul came to Corinth equipped with nothing but the gospel message. Perhaps he had experienced a setback in his own understanding of the gospel. But he came with no excess baggage—just the gospel. He came professing only *Christ, and him crucified.* During his long stay with the Corinthians, he was at times weak and *in fear and in much trembling* (verse 3). Whether this is a reference to physical illness, a form of spiritual depression, or simply a restatement of God's wisdom and humanity's weakness is not clear. But for Paul, this experience indicated the power of God through the gospel.

Paul's speech was not eloquent or wise (verse 4). He confesses later that he is not an impressive speaker (2 Corinthians 10:1, 10). But he seems to be saying far more than that here. He is explaining that when he spoke and taught them the gospel, he was not always clear and understandable. Yet the message was clear. Why? Not because of his fumbling attempts to tell the message, but because God's Spirit and power worked through his best—yet inadequate—statements. The whole experience was a demonstration of God's Spirit and power.

Then Paul concludes with a majestic and bold assertion (verse 5). Their faith has nothing to do with humanity. It does not rest with their own choice to believe or with the eloquence of Paul or Apollos or Cephas. The true message and the faith to believe come from God. What greater assurance could Paul have possibly given them?

§ § § § § § §

The Message of 1 Corinthians 1:10–2:5

These verses introduce the heart of the letter. Paul
knows these believers well. He has lived alongside them
and labored with them. He knows their city, their
influences, and their habits. Having already heard of
existing problems (7:1), and following his careful and full
introduction (1:1-9), he now begins to focus their
attention on Christ. Bringing them to the point of Christ,
he perhaps senses that he will be better able to then
instruct and help them with their tensions and problems.
So, after this refocusing of their faith on Christ, Paul then
diplomatically deals with both their practical questions
(7:1–12:31) and theological questions (13:1–15:58).

§ § § § § § §

1 Corinthians 2:6-16

Introduction to These Verses

Up to this point in the letter, Paul has attempted to explain that the wisdom of humanity is no consequence in the face of God's truth. In fact, human wisdom must be let go, dismissed, released, if the gospel is to be grasped. But once human wisdom is gained, by letting human wisdom die to the gospel, a new, eternally profound wisdom is born.

God's Wisdom Made Known in Christ (2:6-16)

Paul begins by speaking of the *mature*, meaning the mature Christian (verse 6). There is a true and very real wisdom of mature Christians (14:20; Philippians 3:15; Colossians 1:28; 4:12). This deeper wisdom is shared among those who are mature in Christ. What exactly is this wisdom? It is not of this world or of humanity. It is not wisdom of an age or a culture or an insightful ruler. What is it?

Mature Christian wisdom is *secret* and *hidden* (verse 7). Paul does not mean to breed exclusivism. Rather, mature Christian wisdom comes only to those who are known by God. Based on all that Paul has just asserted, maturity in Christ comes from being known by God rather than knowing God. The difference is simple: Because God is in control of the situation—of salvation, of history, of a believer's life—wise maturity results. This wisdom that comes from being known by God is passed on within the

Christian fellowship—it is imparted as Paul says. Thus it is secretive and hidden because it is not human; it rests in and with God. Those who are mature in Christ share this wisdom, a wisdom that is not of the world.

When was this wisdom established? It was decreed before time and Creation *for our glory.* This amazing statement tells us two ways in which Paul must have experienced and therefore understood mature Christian wisdom. On the one hand, because this secret and hidden wisdom is decreed by God before time, Paul is explaining that it was God's plan before Creation. God has a plan. Life at times may seem chaotic and out of control, but God has a plan. This plan is hidden with God and is understood (not known; Matthew 24:36) through fellowship with God.

On the other hand, this plan is for humanity's *glory.* It centers on humanity. Humanity is the peak of creation, the portion of creation chosen for fellowship with God. Glorification of humanity comes only because of this fellowship. And this mature Christian understanding comes through fellowship with God—mature understanding that God initiated.

By the *rulers of this age* (verse 8) Paul is probably referring to evil forces and demonic powers (Ephesians 6:12). These were understood as forces that Jesus constantly contended with (Mark 1:34) and forces that inspired key figures in Jesus' trial and death (Caiaphas, Pilate, and so forth). The rulers of this age could not see beyond the immediate and mundane. They were unable to understand God's plan because of their distance from God. But if they had been near God, the divine secret and hidden wisdom would have been part of their understanding and they would not have crucified Jesus.

By understanding the evil forces and demons in the universe as the reason behind Christ's death, there can be no quesiton as to whether Jesus had to die on the cross. Of course he had to die (Colossians 2:14-15). But the evil forces sought to destroy him, not the individuals in power at the time. Paul is simply saying here that if the persons involved in Jesus' crucifixion had not been driven by evil forces, they would not have sought Jesus' destruction.

In verse 9 Paul gives a somewhat free translation of Isaiah 64:4. This quote affirms and re-presents what Paul has been saying about the wisdom of God and the plan of salvation.

In verse 10 Paul gets more specific, explaining the communion between God and humanity. The Spirit of God or the Holy Spirit is the binding energy between God and humanity. God's Spirit comes upon humanity, revealing God and uniting in communion God and humanity. In this communion, this secret and hidden truth, is communicated the Spirit of God. All of this communion streams from God and not humanity.

In this inter-communion, incomplete or watered-down knowledge is not what is communicated. The Spirit of God *searches everything, even the deep things* (NIV; NRSV= depths) *of God.* It follows that the Spirit communicates not only everything about the creation, but everything of God's truth and plan for the creation. The mature believer is able, through the Spirit and in relationship with God, to gaze into the very essence of God's plan for the universe. What an astonishing assertion by Paul! And yet it must be based on his personal experience, or he could not speak with such certainty and assurance.

Paul turns to an analogy in order to clarify his statements (verse 11). What Paul apparently means by the human *spirit* is something akin to personality or self-consciousness or the inner being of a person. The depth of a person is found in inner thoughts, ambitions, desires, feelings, and so forth. The human *spirit* knows the deep inner person. Applying this idea to God, nothing knows the inner being and depth of God but the

Spirit of God—the Holy Spirit. The Corinthians are interested in *spiritual* things (1 Corinthians 1:7; 12:1-31). So Paul reasons from God and God's inner being to humanity and the Corinthians. The believers in Corinth would have been quick to hear this analogy.

How do persons of faith know the secret and hidden wisdom of God? The answer is clear: by the Spirit of God. Because mature believers receive the Spirit of God, they *understand the gifts bestowed . . . by God* (NRSV; NIV= *what God has freely given us*). Paul does not emphasize the gift as much as an understanding of the gift by the mature Christian. Mature believers see these gifts not as ends in themselves. The mature believer understands them only in relation to the inner being of God.

Even Paul's explanation is beyond words (verse 13). This wisdom about which he speaks does not come from the world or through human wisdom. It comes from the Spirit of God that is of the very inner being and truth of God. The Holy Spirit helps the believer understand profound and divine truths because these believers already have the Spirit.

The person of this world is natural or *without the Spirit* (NIV; NRSV= *unspiritual;* verse 14). The person who is separated from God cannot *receive the gifts of God's Spirit,* and cannot understand them by way of human wisdom and knowledge.

The mature person of God can judge all things or better investigate all things. The same is not true for the person who is separated from God and of this world. The believer's understanding and insight come only from God and cannot be humanly investigated. Therefore the mature person of God has an advantage—but it is not an advantage based on some secret knowledge of God (an idea that was prominent in Gnosticism). The advantage is mature knowledge for all who are in right relationship with God through Christ. Therefore, it is open to all who believe in Jesus the Christ.

Paul again quotes the Old Testament to confirm his reasoning (verse 16). A statement by the prophet Isaiah is summarized (Isaiah 40:13), indicating that humanity can never know the mind of God so as *to instruct him.* However, the Christian has a tremendous advantage. The secret and hidden wisdom of God (verse 7) comes to the believer through Christ. Now the Spirit of God communicates through Christ the very inner thoughts of God.

Paul's summary statement is astonishingly succinct: *But we have the mind of Christ.* Through the deep communications of the Spirit that unite God with humanity through Christ, the mature believer comes to know deeply and profoundly the plan of God. This divine plan has something to do with a humanity that is glorified because God has chosen this species to be in fellowship. Thus humanity is made in God's image. To the non-believer this sounds foolish and mythical. To the mature believer it summarizes some of the deepest and most profound truth of God.

§ § § § § § §

The Message of 1 Corinthians 2:6-16

This section is perhaps second in importance only to Paul's speaking of love (chapter 13). These verses deal with a wisdom that comes only from God, that begins with God's action, and that depends upon God's continued self-revealing for clarity and understanding. This divine wisdom requires the entire Godhead. It implies the need and action of the Father, Son, and Holy Spirit for true wisdom and insight. Only as God draws close to humanity—as God becomes totally human—is humanity able to understand, discern, and be guided. Such is the depth of Paul's teaching.

§ § § § § § §

PART FOUR 1 Corinthians 3–4

Introduction to These Verses

Now that he has explained spiritual maturity in Christ (2:6-16), Paul considers the present spiritual level of the Corinthians. To show his sincere fellowship and camaraderie with the Corinthians, he begins by calling them *brothers*. In the past he could not speak to them as mature believers. They were believers in Christ, but they had not yet grown sufficiently in their new spiritual birth. They still maintained old habits, old ideas, human insights, human values, and human understandings. They had not yet really thought about life and death from God's word spoken in Christ. Hence they were spiritual *infants in Christ.*

Paul's Prior Work in Corinth (3:1-19)

Paul attempted to get them started. He fed them milk because that was all their new faith could accept. Paul sought to inspire them. He worked to keep the Corinthians open to God's truth in Christ through the Holy Spirit. He directed them to wait upon God's influences. At that time, he was unable to give them the heavier food, the solid food of Christian maturity and spiritual wisdom, the profound food that includes the secret and hidden wisdom of God (2:7) and is a gift of God's Spirit. And based on reports he has received (1:11), they are still not ready for this type of food.

Why? Because they are still living life on the basis of

39

human values (verse 3). As long as there is jealousy and competition among them, they are not living out of Christ. When they claim to be followers of certain individuals rather than followers of Christ, they are acting like ordinary people (verse 4).

Then Paul gives a wonderful explanation of the seed growing secretly (Matthew 13:24-30). He begins by asking the true identity of those God has sent to them (verse 5). They are merely servants, or men. Their task is to point people to Christ, and each has a different assignment in the work of the church. Paul came among them initially and spoke the good news. Then came Apollos, reaffirming what Paul proclaimed. But neither Paul nor Apollos gave them spiritual insight and clarity (2:1). Only God can speak and touch the heart of individuals. Only God calls persons to believe. And only God gives growth. So Paul "planted" and Apollos "watered." But it was God who caused the seed of the gospel to take root and grow.

God is everything (verse 7), and those who labor in the Kingdom are equal, or one and the same. Paul again seems sensitive to rivalries and competitions between believers. Payment of the laborers suggests the responsibility of the worker. Because they are paid, they each have a responsibility (and calling) from the Father. Although these workers are equal, because each has been called by God, each receives wages *according to* his *labor*. The wages are spiritual compensations received now and in the life to come. These spiritual compensations differ according to the task, but do fulfill the laborer in accordance with God's call. In this manner, Paul and Apollos are God's fellow workers. Their particular calling makes them fellow workers with God, laboring in the Corinthian field or building.

Christ Is the True Foundation (3:10-23)

Paul now develops this imagery further. His clear intention is to bring everything to the foundation of

Christ. He begins by explaining that only because of God's grace is he a *skilled master builder* (NRSV; NIV= *expert builder*). The grace God gave him enabled him to labor at building a strong foundation. This was all God's doing. Now another is building on the foundation—and so it should be. A foundation is meant to be built upon. All others must take care that the building is in accordance with the foundation. This warning is not only for those who build the community; it is also for those individuals who move ahead and mature in their faith.

There is only one true foundation (verse 11). The church and the individual believer cannot choose any foundation, nor can anyone attempt to establish a substitute foundation. God chose and laid the one foundation, which *is Jesus Christ*. Persons can build on this foundation with worldly human materials. Paul mentions *gold, silver, precious stones, wood, hay, straw*. These items represent often-chosen human values. Paul ends his list with the ridiculous, but all are of the same category: false human desires. All are mundane and far inferior to the foundation of Christ.

Paul grants that some will succeed, as some no doubt have already succeeded at Corinth. Some will build false churches—it is possible. But each person will be known by his or her work, because the work will produce results within and around the believing community. The work will become manifest. And even this truth may be disguised for a time, as perhaps is again already happening at Corinth. But the *Day of our Lord* (1:8; see also Amos 5:18) will eventually expose the false building for what it truly is. These false buildings will be razed with the test of fire or God's final judgment, when things will be seen in relation to the foundation (Romans 2:16).

But those who are faithful to God's word spoken in Christ will be rewarded (verse 14). The reward will be in accordance with the assignment (Matthew 25:14-30; Luke

19:12-27). God will not legally owe them anything for their good work, but they will reap the benefits of being good stewards in that they will always be in right relation with the Master. This is why the amount of the reward is not an issue for Paul. Then Paul adds (verse 15) that if one's work is *burned up*, one *will suffer loss* or lack a right or good relationship with God. The person will not be destroyed or obliterated (he or she *will be saved*), but must pass through the fire of God's judgment because of irresponsible work.

Then Paul refers to the profound status of every believer (verses 16-17). In the Old Testament the Temple was the place where God dwelt in the midst of Israel. Drawing from this imagery, Paul calls every believer *God's temple* because the Holy Spirit dwells within. The foundation of Christ is necessary for the Spirit of God and the Spirit of God is essential for building on the foundation. The holiness of the believers at Corinth is not caused by themselves or based on their accomplishments. Their holiness comes only from God. It follows that because they are holy when they are firmly established in Christ (the true foundation) and so have the Spirit, they will not be destroyed. If anyone attempts to destroy them by leading them away from God or using inferior building material, this false builder will be destroyed (and the false churches will disappear). Or, stated positively, the children of faith will not be separated from God. Based on what Paul has already said, these two verses offer a superb conclusion to his thought thus far.

Now Paul applies his general statements to individuals (verses 18-23). To *deceive* oneself is to think one is wise by using the wrong standards to judge one's wisdom (6:9; 15:33; Galatians 5:3, 7). To think one is *wise in this age* does not mean reliance on human cultural wisdom. Using the standards of the gospel, one must abandon human wisdom and so become a fool according to the world's standards. Then by beginning with God in Christ and learning the ways of God, we become wise following the eternal truth of God. Human wisdom is *foolishness* because it cannot discover or control God (verse 19). Paul then uses two Old Testament quotes (verses 19-20) to affirm his statements (Job 5:13; Psalm 94:11).

The different factions or rivalries among the Corinthian house churches should not boast and claim certain leaders. They have everything. How? Not because of certain leadership; not because of worldly wisdom; not because of life or death; not because of what now is or what is to come. Rather, they have all these things through Christ. They have everything because they finally belong to Christ *and Christ* is *God's*. Through Christ they are held firmly by God.

The Responsibilites of Stewards (4:1-7)

Based on the foundation of Christ, Paul, Apollos, and Cephas should be regarded as builders on the foundation (4:1). Paul is again addressing the factions and rivalries at Corinth. These builders are servants or stewards. They have no value in themselves; their value and importance lie in their calling to establish a solid building on the foundation of Christ. They are stewards or adminstrators of *God's mysteries* (NRSV; NIV= *secret things*). They are teachers and preachers of the gospel, those called to proclaim the secret knowledge of God's purpose. These stewards must be trustworthy or faithful to the mysteries of God (verse 2).

Who can judge such a steward of the gospel? Only God. Paul is not concerned about their judgment, perhaps expressed in their factionalism and rivalries. Their comments do not carry much influence with Paul—he does not not even trust his own conscience. Just because he is currently unaware of any shortcomings from his side, this does not mean he is without fault. He perhaps has unknowingly encouraged rivalries (verse 4). But Paul continually brings everything back to God in Christ. In the end, even if he has made mistakes, God will be the judge. Hence, the Corinthian believers must wait for the Lord (verse 5). Do not get caught up in comparisons, rivalries, and petty judgments. Do not take your eyes off Christ and look judgmentally upon others. Look only to him who will make all things clear. By looking only to Christ, you will see clearly.

Paul now applies his statements to himself and Apollos. He and Apollos are fellow stewards and builders for Christ. They do not get prideful and competitive about whom they have converted or what great work they have accomplished. They do not count numbers of converted persons for self-gain. Rather, they hold to Christ and follow Scripture (the Old Testament). So why should some Corinthian believers think they are better than their neighbors? All are simply sinners saved by the gift of God's grace. Where is there room for pride here?

Paul Admonishes the Corinthians (4:8-13)

Now Paul uses irony to shame the house churches in Corinth. They claim to be filled . . . *rich* . . . *kings* (verse 8). Yet Paul and the other apostles are *last* . . . *sentenced to death* . . . *a spectacle* (verse 9). The apostles have become *fools for* . . . *Christ* . . . *weak* . . . *in disrepute,* and the babes in Christ at Corinth have become *wise in Christ* . . . *strong* . . . *held in honor* (verse 10). The itinerant preachers and teachers have little, and labor with *our own hands* (verses 11-12) as good stewards of the gospel. They *bless* . . . *endure* . . . *answer* (NIV; NRSV= *speak*) *kindly* (verses 12-13). For the gospel's sake, they have become fools, scapegoats, the scum of the earth (Matthew 23:8-12; Mark 8:34-38; 10:42-45). In this sense, their values are of God and not at all the values of humanity. The situation is very ironic. The contrasts are so incredible!

Concluding Admonitions (4:14-21)

Now Paul attempts to put all this in perspective. Why is he speaking so sharply? His purpose is to *admonish* (NRSV; NIV= *warn*, verse 14), to speak as a father who seeks lovingly to encourage positive correction in his children (Romans 15:14; Colossians 1:28; 3:16; 1 Thessalonians 5:12, 14; 2 Thessalonians 3:15). The Corinthians may have many tutors in the gospel of Christ (verse 15). Paul does not question the Spirit's work within the community, raising up guides and spiritual counselors. But the believers at Corinth have few fathers. And Paul is their spiritual father. Through his missionary work, he first proclaimed the gospel to the Corinthians. Even though God brought them to the truth, it was Paul who was called to preach and teach in their midst. In this sense, it was Paul who "fathered" them.

The Corinthians are encouraged to follow the example of their father. Paul, as their father, does not replace the gospel, Christ, God the Father. Rather, Paul is saying that as I live in response to God's grace in Christ, imitate me (11:1; see also Philippians 3:17; 1 Thessalonians 1:6). Live with the same response to God's action in Christ as I seek to do. In order to help them in their imitation of him—and to overcome internal disputes—he will send (or possibly the Greek indicates *has sent*) Timothy, his faithful child in the Lord (verse 17). He will help them focus their attention on Christ, the one foundation of every church.

Paul indicates his plan to visit them. During his lengthy stay at Corinth as a missionary, Paul must have controlled some who desired strong influence over other members. These members are *arrogant,* as though he were not coming to visit (verse 18). But, Lord willing, Paul will come and dissolve their human power and talk so that the churches can be reestablished on the foundation of Christ (verse 20). It is interesting that even under these circumstances, Paul will not come unless the Lord sends him. Then Paul directly challenges them to put things right. What they do with the situation will determine whether his well-intended loving visit will demand gentleness or discipline.

§ § § § § § §

The Message of 1 Corinthians 3–4

Now that Paul had addressed their interests about
deep spiritual wisdom, he turns to the spiritual status of
the Corinthians. He seeks to bring their particular
spiritual interests to the truth of Christ. In this manner
and from a human perspective, he does not scold the
believers at Corinth. Nor does he speak from his own
self-asserted authority. His statements about their
immaturity and need for growth are based solely on the
truth of God spoken in Christ.

§ § § § § § §

1 Corinthians 5–6

Introduction to These Verses

Attention is now turned toward bad habits and questionable living practices. Paul is here addressing the worst of the Corinthian believers' lifestyles. There are problems that have been reported to Paul (1:11). Later Paul will go on to address questions they have asked him. But first things first. Paul has received disturbing news and information. He must deal with these practical problems that will compromise the gospel and could end up destroying house churches at Corinth—and therefore the church at Corinth.

Incest and Excommunication (5:1-13)

First of all, Paul has been told (probably by Chloe's people) that they have an unusual immoral situation in their midst. This situation is so unique that it is not even found among pagans! The Greek word used for this immorality means a type of sexual irregularity and is sometimes translated *fornication*. Because adultery and incest are not mentioned, the irregularity is probably the unusual situation of a man living with his stepmother. And because of the house church members' self-pride in their spirituality, they were obviously ignoring the realm of physical bodily sin (verse 2). Paul argues that spiritual truth must be lived out in the physical world. The believers at Corinth should dismiss these persons from their fellowship and mourn their loss.

Because Paul is not physically with them in Corinth, he has to judge on the basis of being with them in spirit (verse 3). He is not only psychologically with them in spirit, but he is also united to them through the power of the Holy Spirit. In this twofold manner, he judges the situation *in the name of the Lord Jesus* (verse 4). Then Paul instructs that they give the man up to Satan so that the flesh may be destroyed. In this manner, he will be saved! What does Paul mean?

Paul is saying that if this person is delivered into the hands of Satan, Satan will destroy the flesh. But because of Christ's preliminary victory in the cross and resurrection/ascension (15:24-27; Philippians 2:5-11), Satan's authority is now limited and will someday be non-existent. That inward spirit or true essence of this man will not be touched by Satan because Christ binds God and true humanity in Christ eternally. Furthermore, because this man apparently does not wish to reconcile his life with the gospel, the Corinthian believers are to abandon him to Satan so that he will not be encouraged to falsely build his house of straw. Thus the community will not be poisoned and distracted from the foundation of Christ and the guidance of the Holy Spirit.

After showing great concern for the sinful member of the church, Paul turns his attention to the community. He explains that prideful confidence in one's spiritual self affects the entire community (verse 6). The people can have no pride in receiving a gift from God through Christ. Anyway, this spiritual pride leavens the whole lump (Galatians 5:9). In the Jewish community, leaven represented evil (Exodus 12:14-20). The one person living a life of sin affects the whole lump of dough. But if they cleanse out this old evil leaven they will become *a new batch* (verse 7). This cleansing is only possible because Christ is the new Passover lamb already sacrificed for the sins of humanity. Christians now live out a festival of thanksgiving. If the Corinthians seek the unleavened bread of *sincerity and truth* (verse 8), their pride will not get in the way by disturbing God's grace.

The believers at Corinth know better than to *associate with sexually immoral people* (verse 9, NIV; NRSV= *persons*). Paul has already written to them about this danger. (Either this letter is lost to antiquity or a portion remains in Paul's second Corinthians letter; see 2 Corinthians 6:14–7:1.) Of course, they cannot escape from the world (verse 10) in order to avoid sin, but immorality should not be allowed within the community of the faithful. They must associate with those of the world as Jesus did (Mark 2:15). But to allow immoral lifestyles within the community of the faithful is to allow a leaven of evil in the lump that will eventually affect the building up of the community and the maturity of individuals within the community. Further, it means not living a life of thankful response for reconciliation already accomplished in Christ.

Referring again to his previous letter (verse 11; or possibly this letter, see above), he emphasizes that they not associate with immoral individuals within the community. The emphasis is on *brothers*, meaning those within the fellowship of churches. Not even Paul himself can speak or judge those who are outside of the church (verse 12). Only God can judge those outside the community of believers, outside the covenant, those in the realm of Satan. (This is a Jewish understanding; see Deuteronomy 17:2-7.)

Refraining from Lawsuits (6:1-11)

Paul has learned (again, probably from Chloe's people) that a second problem disrupting the church at Corinth has to do with lawsuits. He begins by asking about grievances. We can imagine that Paul is told how one person in the Christian community at Corinth sued another individual either from the same house church or more likely from another house church. Paul is angry. Do

Christians parade their affairs before officials outside the church? Is it not more sensible to deal with such matters internally?

Paul now attempts to admonish and shame them by comparing the heavenly with the earthly (verses 2-6). Christians will be judging the world and angels through the wisdom of God. In the face of such grandeur, can little affairs or disputes in this life between members not be handled easily? Must Christian believers rely upon those outside the church to resolve such matters? Is there no one with any practical wisdom in your midst? Is there no way to keep the dispute internal? Lawsuits between believers is an awful witness to those outside the church. It would be a much better witness to suffer the disturbance or fraud. And to think that Christians would bring a lawsuit against fellow believers! Incredible!

Individuals who pursue such lawsuits against fellow believers are grouped with those associated with sexual irregularity. All these individuals are unrighteous and will have no place in *the kingdom of God* (verse 9). The *kingdom* refers to the future time of blessedness when God will reign supreme and the obstructionist powers of evil will be defeated. Sexual perverts and thieves will not inherit the kingdom of God.

Some of the Corinthian believers had been turned from such behavior when they accepted the gospel (verse 11). Paul states theologically what happened to them. First they were washed clean, being baptized in Christ. Their sins were forgiven and they were brought to God through Christ, cleansed of their rebellious ways. Then they were sanctified, or made holy. The Corinthian believers were put right with God through Christ. Now the Holy Spirit seeks to work in them, building them into holy temples of God. Third, they were justified through Christ and in *the Spirit of our God*. Because they were justified through Christ, they now are being constantly justified or being continually put right with God daily,

1 AND 2 CORINTHIANS

through the Holy Spirit. This is the total gift or salvation package from God. How could the believers at Corinth be prideful and puffed up?

The Root of These Problems (6:12-20)

The main difficulty among the Corinthian believers is lack of firmness in the faith. In order to expose this instability, Paul quotes three sayings that apparently are known by the Corinthians and are perhaps used by individual believers in the house churches (verses 9-11). Paul rightly sees here the beginnings of church fragmentation when groups of believers head off in their own particular biased directions (not unlike today!). To whom or what groups these sayings belonged is now lost to antiquity. But Paul makes it clear with his added brief commentary following each saying that they contain nothing more than human wisdom—certainly they do not contain the wisdom of God.

Paul's conclusion is simple: The body is meant *for the Lord, and the Lord for the body* (verse 13). These sayings do not reflect the giving of our bodies to the Lord in thankful response for the free gift of grace that comes through Jesus Christ. The believer lives physically in thankfulness, trusting in the divine power that raised up Christ and will raise up those who believe (verse 14).

For the remainder of this section, Paul attempts to explain more fully his statements about living in right relationship to God through Christ and in the Holy Spirit. He begins by implying that they surely understand they are in Christ (Romans 12:5; Colossians 1:18). Will they become *prostitutes,* turning to some human source? Paul quickly answers, *Never!* Even Scripture proves them wrong (verse 16, quoting a portion of Genesis 2:24). In contrast, when one is joined to the Lord he or she becomes *one spirit with him* (verse 17). Living on the foundation of Christ means life in the Spirit of God. It means living out of God in response to God.

Thus, believers must literally run from (the meaning of *shun* [NRSV]) sin (verse 18). Paul's next statement in this verse is difficult. He seems to argue that sin of the flesh or sin outside the body of a believer is serious, but it does not change their status before God. That is to say, a believer must seek to continually live in thankful response to God's grace in Christ, but lapses are to be expected (see Romans 7). However, those who do not care to respond to God's grace and so do not rely upon God's grace live in *immorality* (NIV). A perfect example is fornication. This type of continual and perpetual sin changes a believer's status before God. This permanent attitude of sin encourages false covenants based on erotic self-love and disrupts the possibility of true covenants based on self-giving agape love (see chapter 13).

In the form of an easy-to-answer question, Paul repeats (verse 19) what he has said previously (3:16-17). The body of a person houses the temple of God. God dwells in individuals because of Christ's work, sending the Holy Spirit upon them. Now believers no longer stand on their own foundation; they belong to Christ—*You are not your own*. The price of their freedom for God came through Christ's death/resurrection/ascension (verse 20). Their calling now is to *glorify* (NRSV; NIV= *honor*) *God* in thankful response.

§ § § § § § §

The Message of 1 Corinthians 5–6

In this section Paul deals with disturbing information he has received concerning the behavior of some of the Corinthians. The kind of immorality discussed in these verses threatens to destroy both the house churches and the city itself, by compromising the gospel of Jesus Christ. Paul gives both practical and theological advice to the Corinthians on how to respond to these circumstances.

§ § § § § § §

1 Corinthians 7–8

Introduction to These Verses

Paul has just dealt with reports he has heard from
Chloe's people. The reports told of an urgent situation
that demanded Paul's immediate attention. Now he can
turn to other things. Chloe's people also direct to Paul
questions that have surfaced among the Corinthian house
churches. Although two of the topics are vaguely related
to what Paul has just written—marriage and spiritual
gifts—the questions of the Corinthians introduce new
topics into the letter.

Questions About Marriage (7:1-40)

Paul turns his attention to their questions. The
questions had been addressed to Paul in the form of a
letter. This makes Paul's response in letter form
appropriate to the situation. He answers their first
question with no introduction, suggesting that this was a
serious issue among the Corinthians. If Paul's statement
is not in fact their question, we can assume that their
question addressed to Paul was something like the
following: "What type of man/woman relations are
appropriate for the spiritual person?" (Later Paul will
explain his views: verses 25, 32-34.)

Relations between men and women carry temptations
(verse 2). The temptation is to use the relationship for
personal pleasure and gain. Although translation is
immorality, the Greek word is more accurately *fornication*,

indicating a specific issue—sexual irregularity. Apparently loose relations were leading to immoral relations. Paul explains that it is best for each person to have a permanent mate. Such permanence encourages a strong covenant of mutual respectability, dignity, and total love. This type of covenant love reflects the covenant love between God and humanity in Christ through the Holy Spirit.

In this type of mutual love, a person's body is primarily for his or her mate (verse 4). One's body is not for self-indulging, self-seeking pleasure. The body is for giving pleasure to the husband or wife—for giving to another in the covenant of marriage. It also follows that refusal of sexual relations with one's spouse for purely selfish reasons is harmful to the covenant relationship (verse 5). Refusal of intimate relations should be based on mutual agreement for the sake of prayer and fasting, says Paul. But such a time of abstinence must not be permanent or too lengthy, lest temptation become overbearing.

Paul explains that his advice is by *concession* or opinion (verse 6). He cannot command his opinion, he can only command things as he receives them directly from God. These issues demand common sense more than anything. Paul's *wish* (verse 7) is that all were like himself—but he states this in a way that accepts the impossibility of such a wish. What is his state? His state is living a life of obedience to God without having to deal with the complexities of a marriage relationship. Paul has his own special *gift from God*, or calling from God, that of serving God as celibate (see verse 8; also Matthew 19:10-12). Others are called to serve God from within the marriage covenant. (Paul was certainly not negative about marriage; see 11:11-12.)

Up to this point, Paul has been addressing the married people in the Corinthian churches. Now he addresses the *unmarried and widows* (verse 8). He suggests that they would do well to consider staying as they are. This would give them the advantage of being able to concentrate more energy on the foundation of Christ, being built up in the Spirit of God, and living a life of thankful response to God. Of course, because of the human sexual instinct, some have special gifts that will require the companionship found only in the marriage contract (verse 9). Healthy marriage companionship will aid *self-control* and sexual *passion*.

Paul again addresses the married (verses 10-11). Following the teachings of Jesus (Mark 10:2-9), Paul encourages that the marriage covenant should last a lifetime. Jesus saw the marriage contract as a reflection of God's eternal commitment to humanity through Israel. Because God will not break this covenant with humanity through Christ, the marriage covenant between Christians should reflect God's never-failing love and grace.

Then Paul continues with some practical opinions. He points out that the advice he is about to offer is from himself and not from Jesus (verse 12). He encourages any member of the Corinthian churches to remain with an unbelieving wife (and vice versa in verse 13). Paul's emphasis suggests that there may have been a question directed to him from a believer who was married to an unbeliever. Certainly Paul would have had to face this question on many occasions due to the nature of his missionary effort. Paul's concern on the one hand is that believers be a strong witness to Christ, not acting like the pagans or Jews regarding divorce.

On the other hand, Paul was probably aware that unbelievers might come to believe in the Lord through the marriage relationship. A spouse can be consecrated or literally *sanctified* and *made holy* through a mate (verse 14). The believer then brings more to the relationship than the unbeliever. If this holiness or sanctification is not shared through the marriage relationship, the children from the marriage would not have the opportunity to also be sanctified and built up in Christ. Again, the believer brings much more to the relationship than the unbeliever.

However, if the relationship is not sound, let it terminate (verse 15). That is to say, if the unbeliever wants to be free from the relationship, the believer should agree to a divorce. Paul does not use Jesus' teachings in a legalistic manner. Rather, the believer is called to live responsibly and responsively before Christ, in a flexible and open manner.

Christians are called to peace. How? Christ has established true and eternal peace by healing the relationship between God and humanity. This peace filters down to human relationships, being most concentrated in the marriage relationship. If Christians are to pass on this forgiveness and peace (Matthew 18:23-35), the marriage covenant relationship must be honored as fully and as completely as possible. Then Paul asks pointblank, How will they know the eventual eternal status of their spouse? (verse 16). They cannot know! Therefore, struggle to maintain and support the marriage relationship. Hold on to your assignment and calling (verse 17). This is Paul's general rule.

Now Paul applies his general rule (verse 18). If one is called to faith as a Jew (*circumcised*), one stays a Jew as a believer. If one is called as Gentile (*uncircumcised*), one stays a Gentile as a believer. What is really vital is keeping God's commandments and so living a life of thankful response to God (verse 19). The same holds true with marriage (verse 20). The truth of God in Christ surpasses even slave status (verse 21), with the exception of the desire for freedom, which does not apply to the analogy. This is an interesting explanation, because slavery was a much more permanent condition in the social structure of Corinth than marriage (and Paul probably had slave converts in Corinth).

Because Christians are *bought with a price*, new life in Christ must not be restricted by lesser human relationships (verse 23). God's love surpasses human limitations and enables a richer and fuller life beyond human expectation. Christ's work cannot be humanly imprisoned or omitted by any human relationships. So, regardless of the status to which one is called, let the believer be content and *remain* with God (verse 24).

Paul now returns to the unmarried (verse 25; see verses 8-9). The Greek word used in this verse carries the sense of a virgin or young person. Paul explains that he has no direct message from God (in the prophetic sense), but as a true apostle—and by the mercy of God—his insight and words are *trustworthy*. The stage is prepared for a rather direct statement. Paul explains that in light of present circumstances, characterized by Christ's impending return, it is best to keep things as they are (verses 26-27). But if a young virgin or girl should marry, this is acceptable even though life will be more complicated for such a believer (verse 28).

The time is short and Christ's return is near (verse 29). The Corinthian believers are to keep this eternal truth as their deep understanding for daily living. The married are encouraged to see beyond their immediate circumstances, as are those who mourn, rejoice, buy goods, and deal *with the world* (verses 30-31). Our immediate circumstances are transient and momentary. But the time of Christ is for eternity and the fullness of Christ's time has already begun with his death, resurrection, and ascension.

Paul wants the Corinthian believers to focus their attention on the coming Christ (verse 32). If they do, their anxieties will be less. The unmarried man has an advantage, because his focus is concentrated on the Lord's affairs. The married man has to be concerned about marital responsibilities (verses 33-34). The same circumstances apply to the unmarried (virgin) and married woman. Paul's recommendations are based on a sincere interest for the well-being of the believers at Corinth and his desire to have them focus fully on Christ (verse 35).

Regarding premarital sexual relations, Paul suggests that if passions are running high, it is acceptable for persons to go ahead and marry (verse 36). But if possible, it is much better that the persons control their passions and be true to Christ throughout the betrothal period (verses 37-38). All of Paul's advice is offered in the context of the in-between-time of Christ having come and Christ's impending return.

Finally, Paul emphasizes again the permanence of marriage (verses 39-40). His focus here is on the wife who must not leave the husband but who is free to remarry in the event of the husband's death. Paul may be addressing a particular question, or he may have a particular circumstance in mind as he addresses this related issue. If a woman does remarry, she should only do so *in the Lord*. Based on what Paul has said, she is better off staying the way she is. So Paul does accept the possibility of divorce and remarriage under certain circumstances.

Paul concludes his advice with a profound but humble claim. His practical advice has value because his authority is not in himself but in Christ. He has attempted to speak as one who has the Spirit, as one mature and built up in Christ (verse 40).

Concerns About Dietary Practices (8:1-13)

The Corinthians had also asked Paul about dietary habits. Dietary influences would have come from two sources: the Jewish community's kosher habits and pagan religious practices. If food passed through the hands of pagan shopkeepers or merchants, the Jews rejected it because of improper slaughtering and the taint of idolatrous hands. Thus it was already sacrificed for sacred (idolatrous) purposes. Here the Christian community, perhaps influenced by the Jewish community, addresses a similar type of question to Paul: What about food *sacrificed to idols* (verse 1) or tainted by the heathen?

Paul then possibly quotes a portion of the Corinthian letter written to him: All of us *possess knowledge*. By *knowledge* Paul means general understanding. He is not yet referring to true spiritual knowledge (see verse 7). This general human knowledge (about food) makes persons think that they know much and encourages individuals to question others' life practices.

But secular human knowledge is not the best way. A better way is love. Love builds up and encourages sound human relationships. When we imagine we have knowledge, we tend not to accept people for what they are; we see them for what we think they are (verse 2). True knowledge comes from lovingly responding to God; God already knows and loves humanity through Christ (verse 3). In responding lovingly to God through the power of the Holy Spirit, we gain the only true knowledge—knowledge that comes from God and encourages believers to love their neighbors. This true God-based knowledge is not peevish, sulky, or petty. It is genuine, eternal, and essential to our real human nature.

Idols do not really exist (verse 4). Furthermore, Christian believers know there is *no God but one.* Human persons may invent gods and lords for heaven and earth (verse 5). In light of these thoughts, Paul presents the Christian cosmology. The universe has one God called *Father.* Everything exists because of this one Father, and everything exists for this one Father. The connecting link between the one God and the rest of the universe is Jesus Christ. God holds the entire universe together through Christ. Every creature, especialy every human creature, has its purpose, life, and reason for existence only for God through Christ (see John 1:1-5; Colossians 1:15-20).

Not all possess this knowledge of God (verse 7). Some do not look at life in terms of this Christian cosmology. But because some individuals have lived a previous life of idol worship, they feel at times that they are eating food really offered to an idol. They feel guilty. But of course God's love for humanity is not in any way affected by the food we eat (verse 8). Christians are absolutely free from such concern. However, those who have no sense of guilt about food should be sensitive to those who do (verse 9). Be sensitive to the weaker brethren and work to strengthen them and not cause them to stumble.

Consider the practical consequences. If weaker Christians see one more mature in Christ eating in an idol's temple, they will be encouraged to do the same, even though they do not have the deeper knowledge of God in Christ. Even though the more mature believer is not affected, the weaker individuals begin to stumble and perhaps eventually fall from faith—even though these weak persons be those *for whom Christ died* (verse 11). In tempting a fellow believer's weak conscience *you sin against Christ* (verse 12). Then Paul beautifully summarizes his logic with a marvelous and timeless statement so vital for Christian living (verse 13). If something so simple as the food you eat causes a fellow believer to turn from Christ, then eat differently! Or again, never trap and harm new believers so that they lose their way on the journey of faith.

§ § § § § § §

The Message of 1 Corinthians 7–8

In this section Paul addresses practical matters that were on the minds of the Corinthians. He discusses how to live within the marriage covenant, divorce, what unmarried persons should do (those widowed, divorced, or not yet married), how to relate to an unbeliever, and whether to eat food offered to idols. Paul offers all his advice in the context of serving the resurrected Christ.

§ § § § § § §

1 AND 2 CORINTHIANS

1 Corinthians 9:1–11:1

Introduction to These Verses

Paul has been addressing specific questions that the
Corinthian believers directed to him (marriage and food
habits). Before he turns to the area of public worship,
Paul speaks of his own charge to care for the spiritual
well-being of the Corinthians. Paul perhaps senses that
some will take issue with his answers to their questions.
So he speaks of his own authority and he gives the
believers at Corinth some general encouragement.

Paul's Apostolic Responsibility (9:1-11:1)

Paul begins by asking questions that have obvious
answers. The questions are related to previously
addressed issues, but offer a useful guide as to how Paul
perceives the term *apostle*. He argues that because he
lives out what he has stated, he is a good example for
believers. He is *free* for God in Christ and he has *seen
Jesus our Lord.* His seeing Jesus is probably—though not
necessarily—a reference to his Damascus road conversion
experience (see Acts 9:1-22) rather than an observation of
Jesus' earthly ministry. And because the Corinthians are
the fruit of his labors, his *seal . . . in the Lord,* or his
apostolic calling, is very evident (verse 2).

What does it mean to be an apostle? First of all,
apostleship means one is freed in Christ for God; one has
a living relationship with the risen Lord; and the fruits of
one's labor in the Lord are evident. These three

qualifications make Paul a good example for living and an advisor whose authority comes solely from God and not from any human source or self-established authority.

Second, apostleship means being looked after by the believing communities. There are those who would question and examine Paul's authority. Perhaps some questioned whether the church was responsible for the daily maintenance of Paul and other church leaders. Although Paul had supported himself when he lived almost two years in Corinth, he still had the option of community support for *food and drink* (verse 4). And if he had a wife, the same would hold for her. Paul's example of the other apostles and Cephas is interesting, indicating that Peter and many of the other disciples were married and that their wives may have traveled with them. Paul and Barnabas are not an exception. Then Paul adds relevant examples of soldiering, farming, and caring for livestock (verse 7).

Paul does not argue from mere common sense. Even the Jewish law supports his assertions. Quoting the law attributed to Moses (Deuteronomy 25:4), even an ox can eat while it works (verse 9). Mosaic law is for the believer (and not the ox!), so that people will work in the hope of enjoying the fruits of their labor. In this sense, hope is grounded in the end results (in God's plan) and not in the laborer. Spiritual seeds should produce material support for Paul and his colleagues. The Corinthian house churches may have local leaders who deserve this support too—but how much more Paul and Barnabas?

However, if the material needs of Paul and his fellow workers become a stumbling block to the believers at Corinth, he would prefer to not claim this right. Here Paul applies to himself what he has already directed the Corinthians to practice (8:13). Furthermore, even in Jewish practice, those who serve in the Temple or at the altar are supplied with material needs. Following these arguments, Paul makes a statement of fact. During Jesus' earthly ministry he *commanded* that his seventy laborers eat and drink what a household provided for them, because the laborers deserve their wages (Luke 10:1-12).

In light of all this, Paul is not begging. He would rather brag! He cannot brag about his preaching because that is his particular calling from God (verse 16). It was not his choice to preach and his preaching comes from no human source (2:1-5). This burden to preach is captured in Paul's statement, *Woe to me if I do not preach* [NIV; NRSV= *proclaim*] *the gospel!*

Paul is under obligation to no one. But ironically, for the sake of the gospel he limits himself. He is willing to respect any person's values if this will encourage an individual to hear the gospel. Paul gives examples indicating how he has respected Jewish beliefs, the law, Gentile values, and weakness of conscience in order to *save some* (verse 22). This suspension of his own needs and interests allows him to better fulfill his calling and thereby *share in its blessings* (verse 23).

The city of Corinth knew well the games of Olympia. This ancient Greek city, less than one hundred miles west of Corinth, included a Greek temple and game sites. The Greek games included boxing and wrestling, racing on foot, horse and chariot racing, throwing the discus and javelin, and other events. Relying upon their familiarity with the Olympic games, Paul speaks of competing in a race. Christianity is like racing: By entering the race one does not automatically receive a prize. Rather, one has to run well to win. Athletes train, discipline themselves, and control their desires, all for a worldly prize. The believer runs the race of faith for eternal prizes.

Have a purpose in running, suggests Paul (verse 26). Discover your calling from God. Learn of the gifts God has given you. And use these gifts to the best of your energies. Do not let your habits disqualify you and ruin your race. A true and proper response to God's grace in Christ is to do your best. This does not mean, for Paul, that the believer is earning God's love and attention and that the race must be won if a blessing of grace is to be received. Rather, the race is a thankful response to God's grace. "So run your best!" says Paul.

But there is another danger besides the danger of being disqualified from the race. There is the danger of overconfidence. *Our forefathers* (NIV; NRSV= *ancestors*) probably refers to the majority of early believers who were primarily Jewish (10:1). In contrast, Paul's audience in Corinth was primarily Gentile. So Paul explains how the early Jewish believers had a great deal to be confident about. Their ancestors experienced the Exodus, they *were baptized into Moses* (see Exodus 16:4-35), and they were fed *spiritual* (supernatural) food and drink (verses 3-4). They experienced the signs that anticipated the coming of Christ. They drank from the same hand of God that produced God's full word spoken in Christ. The Jewish people had all these advantages, and yet they lost the race! Many of these early believers stumbled, fell, and perished in the wilderness (Numbers 14:16). So do not be overconfident. Just as God was not pleased with the early Israelites because they began to trust in themsleves and not in God, neither would God be pleased with believers at Corinth who trusted merely in themselves.

Paul now gives a catalogue of errors that led to the Jewish troubles in the wilderness (verses 6-13). Those at Corinth should heed the warning and seek to avoid these traps and pitfalls as they travel in their particular wilderness of life. The traps include idol worship (Exodus 32:4-6), immorality (Numbers 25:1-18), testing God to do our will (Numbers 21:5-6), and general grumbling and complaining (Numbers 16:14, 49).

In this critical time of final adjustments and developments, be careful not to fall. If you think you are standing, you are trusting in yourself—and you will fall. Be careful! The temptations are the same from age to age and generation to generation. But temptation is not the emphasis here. God is the important and vital factor in the faith that has been given you. *God is faithful,* and so will protect believers from too powerful a force that would tempt them away from God. And in the face of any negative force, God will provide the manner in which to overcome the temptation.

Paul now focuses his attention on idolatry. Perhaps there was a special problem in the Corinthian churches that involved a form of idolatry. Or perhaps Paul simply sees this as a particularly dangerous temptation in light of Israel's troubles. In any case, Paul tells the Corinthians to run away from any form of idolatry. Appealing to their common sense and good judgment, Paul explains that idols remain at a distance from the worshiper. But when Christians share in the cup of communion, they actually become a part of *the body of Christ* (verse 16). Christ's blood and body represented in the wine and bread unite all together in one body.

Paul again uses the Old Testament to explain Christian truths. Because the priests (Leviticus 10:12-15) and worshipers (1 Samuel 9:10-24) of the old covenant on occasion consumed the sacrifice, they were united with God and shared spiritual blessings. In this context, the food offered to idols and the dead idols themselves represent nothing but demons and things that seek to obstruct the very will of God. Believers cannot worship God and demons.

Paul again quotes a saying that perhaps was familiar to the Corinthian believers (verse 23). The phrase at the end of his earlier statement, *I will not be mastered* [NIV; NRSV= *dominated*] *by anything* (6:12), is now changed to *not all things build up* (NRSV; NIV= *not everything is constructive*). Echoing Jesus' words (Mark 12:29-31), Paul tells them not to be self-centered or preoccupied with their own spirituality, but to help their neighbors and seek to build up the community. As long as they are in communion with God, God's strength protects them from having to worry about food from the marketplace that has been dedicated to idols. Quoting Psalm 24:1, Paul encourages believers not to worry when they dine at a non-Christian's home.

However, if they are told that the food was *offered in sacrifice*, they should not eat. The reason is not to protect their own consciences—the believers are already protected by God's strength and truth in Christ. They should refuse for the sake of the non-Christian believer; refuse so that they are witnesses to the living and resurrected Christ. Anyway, the person who is free in Christ should not allow a non-believer to determine how he or she lives. Living habits must be determined only in relation to Christ and as a witness to Christ.

Paul then concludes his statements about food and idols. *Whatever you do,* make sure God gets the glory. And in glorifying God, do not trip others on their spiritual journey through the wilderness. Do not offend the Jews or the Gentiles and their laws of eating and drinking. Also, do not offend the church, the various house congregations—each other!

§ § § § § § §

The Message of 1 Corinthians 9:1–11:1

The believer's sole task is being a witness, pointing with all of life's living habits to the truth of God in Christ. Thus the true believer pleases all, not for self-glorification, but that all may come to know Christ.

In this manner, they should follow Paul's example. Paul does not mean that they should in any way glorify him. Rather, as Paul centers his life and activities on the living and resurrected Christ, they should do the same. They should imitate Paul in their lifestyle and habits, including food and drink. By following Paul, they will focus their full life on Christ—and not Paul.

§ § § § § § §

1 Corinthians 11:2–12:31

Introduction to These Verses

The central activity of the believers at Corinth was worship. Paul almost certainly would have received news from Chloe's people about house churches at worship. Perhaps he also has been asked direct quesitons about women in worship, the celebration of the Lord's Supper, and the place of spiritual gifts.

Men and Women in Public Worship (11:2-16)

Paul begins this difficult topic by praising the believers at Corinth. The believers *remember* him by showing respect for the work and teachings he has delivered to them. They *maintain the traditions* (NRSV; NIV= *holding to the teachings*) of the gospel, holding fast to the essential truths of Christianity. At this point, there was no official written summary of the Christian faith. The gospel was passed orally from proclaimer to convert. The Corinthians are respecting Paul's essential message.

However, as they maintain the tradtions, they should understand that there are certain basic Christian structures and truths. God is the divine source behind all things. So Paul reasons from God by beginning with Christ—and not man, or Adam. In this manner, Paul begins with the first real man in God rather than the first fallen man distant from God.

In verse 3 Paul introduces two important and somewhat contrasting thoughts. They are developed throughout this section and characterize Paul's overview of the Christian faith at this point in his life. Because he attempts to weave these ideas together, these verses are very complicated and sometimes difficult to follow. This whole section moves along on two general thoughts.

Paul's first point is indicated in his use of the term *head*. In Greek thought, *head* carries the meaning of *origin* or explanation of something. In the context of Paul's rabbinical background and training, the term carries the meaning of origin as determined by God. The head of something explains God's purpose for that person or thing. Based on the second Creation account, woman has her origin and explanation from man. This idea creates a hierarchy of natural authority in the creation.

However, Paul's second point does not accept a created natural order of authority in the creation. His second point is indicated in the term *husband* (NRSV; NIV= *man*; the same Greek word means *husband* or *man*), but is found throughout the contrasts in this verse. He stresses here a covenant-type relationship between two parties. The covenant relationship implies mutuality and inner necessity. Both sides in a covenant relationship need each other to be complete and wholesome. It is in the covenant established in Christ that all humanity is equal. In Christ, there is no hierarchy (see Galatians 3:28). Christ has reconciled all to the Father. Christ alone has the authority and all are equal in him.

So for Paul, the basic Christian understanding of the creation structure is a natural hierarchy of authority *and* the equality of all. Everything is God-determined and only makes sense in relation to something else. Verse 3 could be paraphrased as follows: Christ is the origin of man and so covenanted to man in binding relationship (see 8:6); man (*her husband*) is the origin of woman and so covenanted to woman in binding relationship; God is the origin of Christ and the two are covenanted together for the reconciliation of the creation.

From this understanding, Paul draws certain conclusions. First of all, with regard to the man, Paul concludes that praying and prophesying in the Christian assembly with a veil or a cap disgraces his origin, Christ. In antiquity, a head-covering (not a veil) signified freedom, or freedom for something. In contrast, a bare head signified servanthood. With regard to man, then, Paul seems to be suggesting that all men have their origin and explanation in Christ and therefore are servants of Christ (7:21-23; 2 Corinthians 4:5). In this manner, the uncovered head reflects the binding and covenanted glory of Christ (2 Corinthians 3:18).

Now Paul turns to woman, and this is where the controversy supposedly begins (verse 5). But if we remember that Paul is attempting to speak on two levels, there is less controversy than we might think. In fact, the deeper question is whether Paul can successfully make his point by holding these two thoughts together (a created hierarchy of order and a covenant relationship of equality). But for Paul, these are two facts of the basic traditions or structures of the universe. Now, how does Paul relate this to woman and public worship?

We should begin by noticing that according to this verse women did pray and prophesy during public worship in the house churches of Corinth. The active participation of women is why Paul needs to address the issue. So Paul is not forbidding nor rejecting activity that is already in practice. Based on the covenant relationship established between God and humanity in Christ, Paul could not have argued otherwise, because all are equal in Christ. Rather, his intention is to merely regulate how it is to be done. What are the criteria for regulating this practice? Based on Paul's understanding of the structures of creation, women are different from men. Therefore, they should appear in the public assembly differently from men. Men should not cover their heads. Women should wear veils. In Christ there is no distinction. In the hierarchical orders of creation, a distinction is necessary.

Paul's natural order of creation is further emphasized when he refers to shaving the head. On the one hand, the shaved head was a sign of disgrace in the Hellenistic world. For Paul, then, the woman who appears in public worship without a veil disgraces herself with regard to the natural order of things. On the other hand, the natural distinction between a man and a woman suggests the need for a natural distinguishing feature. Even though man and woman stand together and are equal in Christ, they are created differently by God at the beginning of time.

Man is the *image and glory* [NIV; NRSV= *reflection*] *of God* (verse 7). Based on Genesis 1:26, Paul explains that man is created for fellowship, companionship, and communion with God. This is God's choice, not man's. This situation reflects man's *image and glory* as a special creature of God. But then Paul adds that *woman is the glory* [NIV; NRSV= *reflection*] *of man.* Here Paul draws from a second Creation account found in Genesis 2:18-23. Drawing again from his rabinnical training, he explains that a woman is created as a partner of man from the rib of Adam. So, from the order of creation, there is a natural difference between man and woman. This natural difference agrees with his point above, that *the husband is the head of his wife* (verse 3, NRSV; NIV= *man*).

Continuing his reasoning from the natural order of things, Paul introduces the idea of angels. The phrase *symbol* [NRSV; NIV= *sign*] *of authority* in verse 10 has traditionally been translated *veil.* How are these thoughts of angels and authority to be understood? The term *angels* is most likely a reference to God's appointed workers who are meant to guard (with authority) the order of things or the structure of creation. In Genesis 6:1-4, angels are referred to as *sons of God* who *saw that they were fair* and took advantage of them. So the veil has

1 AND 2 CORINTHIANS

a double meaning. On the one hand and in accordance with the natural order, the veil is a sign of modesty, hiding woman's natural attractiveness. The veil is a natural covering that helps the public worship focus on God and nothing else. On the other hand and in accordance with equality in Christ, the veil identifies the covenant partner of man (Galatians 3:28).

Paul's argument is an attempt to move from theology to practicality. He begins by reasoning from God. Community worship is for the glorification of God. But, because women in Corinth do participate in worship, a sign of their place in the creation and of their new status in Christ is necessary. The veil is the answer. In the past, women had no authority in worship—especially in Judaism. Because this is now changed, Paul seems to want to give the veil a double meaning of covering man's glory (the attractiveness of women) and symbolizing woman's place of authority and equality through Christ in the body of the church.

Now Paul emphasizes covenant equality in Christ rather than the order of authority in the creation. *In the Lord* (verse 11) or in Christ man and woman cannot be distinguished. In the created order they are different. In Christ they are one, and not independent. At Creation, woman came from man; now man is born of woman. Such is the binding relationship that is only realized in Christ who heals the broken relationship between God and humanity. This healed divine/human relationship is reflected and witnessed in the man/woman relationship. Thus all human beings are equal in Christ.

Paul then turns to the issue of a woman's dress in worship. Once again, he argues from the level of the natural order. Be sensible about all this, Paul says, asking what is *proper for a woman*. The expected answer to the question he asks is no. The created natural structure of the universe (see Romans 1:26-27 for a further Pauline commentary on the natural order) designates a basic difference between men and women. This difference is visibly clear in the natural length of hair that is assigned to each gender from Creation. (The Roman Stoic philosopher of the first century A.D., Epictetus, argued that hair on the chin was a natural distinction between a man and a woman.)

Paul concludes his complicated discussion of this topic rather abruptly. If the Corinthians wish to argue over this rather trivial point, they should remember that he—and his fellow workers and the church generally—do not endorse other habits. Paul's two thoughts (see verse 3) can be combined and summarized by saying: The best witness to Christ is to follow nature. This is Paul's solution to their difficulties. Still, they must decide for themselves. But at least they know where Paul (and Christ's church) stands on this issue—theologically and therefore practically.

Practicing the Lord's Supper (11:17-34)

Now Paul turns to a far more serious issue. His information about the Corinthian habits is probably based on reports from Chloe's people. Paul indicates his concern about this issue with his opening words. Paul cannot *commend* or *praise* them for this issue. He would like to, but he cannot. In fact, based upon reports he has received, the believers at Corinth are spiritually hindered by their assembly for worship. This bold assertion suggests Paul's deep concern over the manner in which they celebrate the communion meal at worship. For Paul, the Lord's Supper is the key element in worship.

The information Paul has received has yet to be verified. But it is such a scandalous report that Paul says he partly believes it. No one would invent such a report. First of all, there are divisions or diverse group attitudes among the believers. The very fact that these different attitudes or divisions exist suggests that at least some are genuine in their faith, clinging to Christ alone. With this

1 AND 2 CORINTHIANS

state of affairs, the Corinthian believers are certainly not coming together as one body or fellowship in Christ when they think they are eating the Lord's Supper. Because of their divisions, they are not honoring but slandering Christ.

What are these different divisions? The divisions include differing attitudes about the Supper based on class distinction and possibly kosher foods. The believers are not eating the Lord's Supper because they do not hold to ceremony. Rather, each person is eating as he or she wishes. Some people are going hungry because others eat everything; and others drink so much they are drunk in the assembly of worship.

Having repeated what he has heard, Paul's immediate response is disbelief: *What!* Can this be? (verse 22). People should take these attitudes about the Lord's Supper and practice them in their own homes. These attitudes are not right for Christ's church in worship. And Paul will not commend them for practicing the Lord's Supper because these very attitudes suggest they are not communing together and they are not communing in the Lord.

Paul's previous instruction about the Lord's Supper was directly from the Lord. How Paul received this tradition from the Lord is not clear. Was Paul an eyewitness of Jesus and his ministry? Did Paul receive this information from one who was an eyewitness? One of the original disciples? Did Paul receive this information on the Damascus road? As we noted earlier, Paul was probably not an eyewitness of Jesus, or he would have argued this in support of his apostleship. It is most likely that Paul received this information from one of the original disciples and then had his understanding further confirmed by the living Lord.

In any case, Paul gives the Corinthians a summary of what he has taught them in the past. These words quoting Jesus form the oldest written tradition known for instituting the Lord's Supper. The Gospels of Matthew (26:26-29), Mark (14:22-25), and Luke (22:14-20) follow Paul's words, suggesting that this tradition comes from the disciples. We should recall that Paul's statements describe Jesus' action with the disciples on the night before Passover. The Passover festival celebrated Israel's deliverance from Egypt. The celebration centered on a sacrifical lamb that was offered to God. In this context, Jesus' words take on a deep meaning which the Corinthians seem to have forgotten in the midst of all their infighting and silly practices. The Supper is for the *remembrance* of Christ and his work; it is a memorial that recalls his lamb-type sacrifice that delivers humanity from rebellion and self-destruction.

The cup carries the same significance as the bread. As the bread represents Christ's body, so the cup represents the new covenant sealed in his blood. The bread (Christ's body) represents the main meal; the cup is the drink that confirms and finalizes the meal. Thus the cup seals the covenant established by the sacrifice of Christ's flesh (see Exodus 24:8; Jeremiah 31:31-34). Paul concludes by explaining the purpose of this memorial. Whenever the Corinthian believers share in the Lord's Supper, they bear witness to the truth of Christ. And they are called to be witnesses until *he comes* (verse 26; 15:23-25).

Having stated the rumored practices of the Corinthians and the correct meaning of the Lord's Supper, Paul makes an obvious conclusion. The person who wrongly practices the Lord's Supper is guilty of making Christ's sacrifice for the deliverance of humanity null and void. Do not lapse into bad habits. This is the center of worship. Approach it cautiously by first examining the self so the Supper will truly be a witness to the living and resurrected Christ. But if a person partakes of the Lord's Supper without realizing that the food signifies the body and blood of Christ, that person brings judgment upon himself or herself—eternal judgment.

This eternal judgment works itself out in practical ways. In Paul's day, it was thought that demons were the cause of sickness, mental illness, and sometimes death (10:20). There were those present in the fellowship who were *weak and ill* (NRSV; NIV = *sick*). Some even had died, or *fallen asleep* (NIV; NRSV = *died*; see 15:6, 20). Paul uses this fact as a warning that the Lord's Supper be practiced properly and correctly. If believers perceive the true spiritual meaning of the Supper, and examine themselves in Christ before partaking, they cannot be *judged* because they will be right with God in the covenant of Christ. But then again, Paul seems to add, almost as an afterthought, when God does judge us, God disciplines us so we will not fall (verse 32).

Then Paul concludes his instruction and comments. His concern is that they *wait for one another*. Eat the meal together as a fellowship, remembering Christ's life and work. If it is food you want, eat at home. Otherwise, you destroy the meaning of the Lord's Supper. And there are other problems in the Corinthian practice of the Lord's Supper that he will give directions about later. But this more important error of division and attitude had to be dealt with immediately.

Comments About Spiritual Gifts (12:1-31)

Now Paul turns to the third topic of concern related to public worship. How are *spiritual gifts* or spiritaul persons to be understood? Whether Paul had heard this from Chloe's people or whether they had asked Paul this quesiton is not certain. But Paul does not want the Corinthians to be uninformed about this matter. Some Corinthian believers had worshiped idols, proving that their apparent spirituality was exclusively self-motivated. But be assured that Christian spirituality does not come from self or any other source. Because the Spirit of God comes through Christ, no believer could ever say "Jesus be cursed" (verse 3). But the opposite is also true. No unbeliever could ever say "Jesus is the Lord" without the guidance of the Holy Spirit. Paul's test of spirituality is clear: Everything comes from God and returns to God through Christ in the Spirit.

All the different gifts of God come through the same Holy Spirit. The source is the same; the gifts must be seen from God's perspective—not the perspective of humanity. These gifts indicate types of service in the Lord. So gifts and service are bound together just as the Holy Spirit and Christ are bound together. And as Christ and the Spirit are God's message to humanity, so a believer's gifts and service enable a Christian to live out a thankful response to God. For Paul, the threefold God (trinity) means a threefold experience in the life of the believer. This threefold response of gift, service, and thanksgiving is given for one purpose, that of upbuilding the community of faith.

From the source of the Spirit come diverse gifts: *the message* (NIV; NRSV= *utterance*) *of wisdom* and *knowledge* (verse 8), referring to practical discourses, teaching, and counseling; gifts of *faith,* or strong members witnessing to the source of the community; *healing,* both spiritual and physical; gifts of the working of miracles, *prophecy,* spiritual discernment, various kinds of *tongues,* and *interpretation of tongues* (verse 10). These gifts are apparently known by the Corinthian believers. The one Spirit of God gives these gifts, not in accordance with humanity's desires, but in accordance with God's will and for the health of the community.

Why does the Spirit give diverse gifts? Paul uses the analogy of the body to explain how the Spirit comes from God and gives gifts to persons in accordance with God's will (not humanity's). A body is unified but has several parts. The many individuals of the body of Christ are not only unified in Christ but receive from Christ through the Spirit an assigned gift and place of service. The Spirit comes from God. Believers baptized into one body drink the same Spirit. This is the unity and diversity of Corinth's house churches.

Paul pushes this analogy further. The nature of a body is a unity of many parts. On the one hand, one part cannot justly say that because it is not some other part of the body it does not belong. Perhaps some house church members in Corinth were arguing and competing over certain tasks and responsibilities within the community. On the other hand, everyone cannot be one part of the body. This would deny the very nature of body. Rather, the body is naturally created and ordered by God.

So it is with the church, the body of Christ. The many are in the one. Parts of the body do not have the natural or spiritual right to discharge or cut off any other part of the body. The parts of the body that have the hidden and most discreet gifts have, in fact, the most important gifts. It is not the most visible gifts that are of the greatest importance to the community, such as speaking in tongues. The showiness of certain gifts indicates that they are the least important. Perhaps Paul is remembering certain individuals who had promoted such thinking among the house churches in Corinth. Paul is quite clear that the lesser gifts receive greater honor in the assemblies and the unpresentable parts are treated with greater modesty (verses 23-24).

God's creation of the body has a beautiful naturalness. The weaker and humbler parts are in fact the stronger because, as with Paul, God is made strong in weakness (2 Corinthians 12:10). This naturalness keeps strife from entering the body. There is no competing or struggling in the body because each part knows its gifts, its place of service, and its means of thankful response to God. The elimination of competition allows for an environment of caring, concern, and upbuilding. What happens to one happens to all—good or bad.

What does all this mean? Paul explains what he has been trying to say in a summary paragraph (verses

27-31). The Corinthian believers are *the body of Christ* collectively and individually (verse 27). Paul now lists God-ordained assignments in order of importance (see Ephesians 4:11-16): apostles (or preachers), prophets (also proclaimers of the gospel), teachers, miracle workers, healers, helpers, administrators, and those who speak in tongues. Then Paul asks if all could do one task, or if all should be the same. Of course not! They should struggle and seek the *greater gifts,* or the gifts that have less showiness. According to Paul's ordering, at least some Corinthians sought the lowest gift of all, that of speaking in tongues. Value those higher gifts on my list, says Paul. From this discussion, Paul launches into a profound statement about the gift of God to humanity. God's gift exceeds all gifts of the Spirit. God's gift is the gift of love. The gift of God is *a still more excellent way* (NRSV) or *the most excellent way* (NIV).

§ § § § § § §

The Message of 1 Corinthians 11:2–12:31

In this section Paul continues to address concerns that have evidently been raised by the Corinthians. Here he discusses the place of women in worship, the celebration of the Lord's Supper, and the varieties of spiritual gifts. Spiritual gifts lead Paul to a summary statement concerning the gift God has given to humanity.

§ § § § § § §

1 Corinthians 13

Introduction to These Verses

Now that Paul has given some practical directives, he can speak with greater freedom and broader theological insight. In this chapter Paul discusses the better way or the way of love.

The Superiority of Love (13:1-13)

The manner in which Paul formulates his *more excellent way* has been called a hymn of love, even though it is prose and not poetry. In the first three verses of this section, he contrasts gifts and other actions of the religious instinct with the gift of love. Paul himself experienced the gift of tongues (14:18), which he has just placed last in his list of spiritual gifts (12:10). So he can rightly use himself as an example. If he speaks in *tongues* but does not have love, he is nothing more than an annoyance to others. What is Paul attempting to say here? The key to his opening statements and to this whole section is the word *love*.

The Greek word Paul uses for love throughout this chapter is very important. The word *agape* is not a common term in ancient Greek. The more common Greek term is *eros* (sexual desire), which is the root of the term *erotic*. Paul's use of *agape* for love indicates his concern and intention to communicate a deeper meaning of the term for the Corinthians. Following all that Paul has previously written in his letter to these believers, his understanding of the term *love* comes solely from God.

The *more* or *most excellent way* (12:31) is God's way. God elected Israel to be the chosen people, God's instrument to prepare the way for the plan of salvation. That plan has reached initial completion in Christ, who has defeated the powers of darkness, rebellion, and desertion. Now humanity can freely respond thankfully and worshipfully to God's love. Agape love is given by God for the sake of humanity, risking humanity's rejection and denial.

What then holds and indeed draws humanity to God? For Paul, it is *agape*, divine love. God's love is more powerful than anything else. This love binds humanity to God through the self-giving love expressed in Christ. The Lord came, suffered, and died so that all persons will now have the opportunity to freely respond to God's love. How powerful is this agape love? It is more powerful than the Corinthians think and can even imagine! It is more powerful than laws, legal requirements, stated obligations, threats, demands—or any other non-loving set of rules or show of force. God risks everything. But the binding force of that agape love is more powerful than anything else in the universe (Romans 8:37-38). Nothing can match the power of God's love. Consequently, humanity is eternally bound to God in Christ through the Spirit.

From humanity's side, agape can only be defined by God's character made known in Christ. Humanity cannot define the term as used by Paul. Perhaps this is why he has chosen such an unusual term to identify and describe the more excellent way. In essence, Paul understands agape as the primary and only real divine attribute (see 1 John 4:8, 16). Then Paul goes on to explain how this agape love should be reflected in the lives of Christian believers.

Paul explains that if believers do not reflect God's

love, they do nothing more than make hard, loud sounds (like *gongs* and *cymbals*). In the worship gatherings of communities or various house churches, believers should reflect God's agape love among fellow believers. This is far more important than speaking in the *tongues of men* (NIV; NRSV= *mortals*) (ordinary speech) *and of angels* (ecstatic speaking in tongues). Christians are called to reflect the very love of God in their lives. This love has been made known fully in Christ. One of Jesus' primary teachings on this subject is the parable on forgiveness, Matthew 18:21-35.

Even if the Corinthian believers have powers of prophecy, but do not reflect divine love, they are empty. Here Paul mentions one of the higher gifts on his list (12:10), a gift relating to the higher mysteries of God's truth. But for Paul, the much deeper mystery and far greater truth—greater than profound prophetic pronouncements—is the mystery that God freely chose humanity for eternal fellowship. As a result, God loves the Corinthians and has acted out that love in the birth, life, death, and resurrection/ascension of Christ.

Even if the worst possible disasters could happen to a person, nothing is gained without agape love. Paul here uses the term *gain* (verse 3). Regardless of how much the Corinthian believers give away and give up, they cannot add anything to their salvation in Christ. Do not trust in self-sacrifice. Rather, put your trust only in the sacrificial love of Christ.

In verses 4-7 Paul contrasts divine love with human love. The type of agape love made known or revealed in Christ is patient and kind. These expressions of divine love in Christ bear witness to God's attributes of wisdom and grace. This true nature of God made known in Christ should be reflected in the Corinthian believers. Like their God, love in the midst of their community should be *patient* and *kind*, certainly *not envious, boastful* (bragging about achievements), *arrogant* or *proud* (of self), stubborn about having its own way (verse 5), or *rude* (dwelling on feeling hurt).

Nor does this agape love wish evil and misfortune on others. Rather, agape love reflecting God's love for humanity can only sincerely rejoice when others do well or experience good fortune. As the divine love of God has borne all the rebellion of humanity in Christ, so believers should bear and withstand all things. Bear what? Because the general context is one of love in relationships, Paul is speaking here about the attitude and fellowship among the Corinthian believers. Agape love bears or conceals what is pleasing in others. At the same time, agape love believes in others (both in and outside of the fellowship) as children of God, *hopes* in the ultimate destination of others as eternal dwellers with God, and endures the temptation to regress and live a human eros-type love.

In the last group of verses (verses 8-13), Paul contrasts agape love with other gifts of the Spirit. There is only one divine truth that will endure and never end. It will never end because it is God's free will that is expressed in agape love. God's will is to fellowship with humanity for eternity and Christ has acted out God's will. Nothing can reverse this act. This agape love will never end.

But other things will end. Prophecies will end because God's work at a particular time and place will be fulfilled. Those who speak in tongues will someday stop because of their passing on to full fellowship with God in eternity. The knowledge of God will pass away when God is fully revealed in Christ's second coming.

For now, we are all little children. Paul's use of the term *child* does not reflect immaturity as much as naivete or a sense of not yet being fully aware. Thus speaking, thinking, and reasoning are now done without full awareness and maturity. However, someday the believers in Corinth will outgrow these limitations and restrictions.

To explain this further, Paul uses the contrast of looking in a mirror. Because ancient mirrors were sometimes rather crude, Paul's statement probably had more meaning to the Corinthians than for the reader of Paul's letter today. Nevertheless, the contrast is an enduring one. The limitations of our own body are similar to looking in a dim mirror. But someday, we shall be *face to face* with God. Now our present knowledge is partial, but someday it will be full. How full will that knowledge be? Our knowledge will be as complete as God's present knowledge of us.

So Paul concludes his explanation of the more excellent way. *Faith* is certainly necessary. Faith is based in God and is a gift of God. Faith is necessary if one is to be a Christian. Faith is based in God and is the manner in which a person comes to know God's ways, works, and will. *Hope,* like faith, is also based in God and receives its meaning and purpose from God.

§ § § § § § §

The Message of 1 Corinthians 13

For Paul, the greatest way is agape love. This love is first and foremost God's love for humanity. God freely chooses to be in fellowship with humanity in Christ. Humanity deserves nothing, earns nothing, achieves nothing. But God freely loves humanity. Because God loves humanity, humanity is reconciled to God and freed to live a life of thankful response to God. Loving God means loving one's neighbor.

§ § § § § § §

1 Corinthians 14

Introduction to These Verses

Now that Paul has established the base of all creation—agape love—he turns to other gifts. These other gifts were probably very interesting to the Corinthians.

Speaking in Tongues (14:1-40)

Paul explains that the Corinthians' primary goal should be reflecting the agape love of God in their lives and fellowship. If you do this, then and only then should you *eagerly desire* (NIV; NRSV= *strive for*) other gifts, such as prophecy. Paul first uses the word *prophesy* in terms of speaking in tongues, explaining that this type of prophecy gives praise to God (*mysteries in the Spirit*), but is not useful for the community of fellowship (verse 2). Now Paul uses the term as a means of *upbuilding* [NRSV; NIV= *strengthening*] *and encouragement* for the community of believers, such as explaining and helping fellow believers in the fellowship.

Prophecy as speaking in tongues uplifts only the self; prophecy as exhortation uplifts everyone. Paul wishes they could all be uplifted by speaking in tongues, but the more important type of prophecy is to upbuild the community of faith. The one exception is when a person interprets the speech, bringing a message of upbuilding for the entire community of faith. Paul's overriding concern is spiritual benefits for all believers of the church.

The situation at Corinth concerning speaking in tongues must have been serious. Even though Paul has clearly argued his point, he continues his discussion. Using himself as an example, he argues that prophecy (as encouragement and upbuilding) is the only sensible way he could help them. In this manner, he can bring them a *revelation* concerning the last days, *knowledge* concerning God's truth, and *instruction* (NIV; NRSV= *teaching*) or *prophecy* concerning Christian living. Paul's argument is further illustrated by using the musical instruments of *harp, flute,* and *bugle* (verses 7-8, NRSV; NIV= *trumpet*). Unless the notes are clear and intelligible, how can they be understood?

The implications are clear. If some Corinthian believers use unintelligible speech, how can anyone understand and gain from such a gift? Unless words have meaning, they vanish in the air when they are spoken. Paul suggests that anyone who speaks in tongues should try and help the community by praying for an interpreter (verse 13). *Five words* that help the other members of the fellowship or community are better than any number of words that cannot be understood (verse 19).

Paul now redirects the argument but with the same intention. The believers at Corinth must not be immature in their understanding of the faith (verse 20). Quoting the prophet Isaiah (28:11-12), Paul explains that when God spoke to believers in a foreign tongue (in this case, that of the Assyrians), Israel would not listen. In the same manner, tongues do not help anyone but the speaker. Tongues can only be a sign for unbelievers or for those who do not understand. In contrast, prophecy as encouragement for the community is clearly a sign for believers.

If all church members came together and spoke in tongues, what kind of witness would this be to Christ? Everybody would be speaking his or her own tongue and no one would understand. This defeats the very purpose of the community. In contrast, if an unbeliever or outsider hears prophecy that upbuilds, encourages, and expounds the truths of the faith, the outsider will hear the witness and be drawn to the truth. The conscience or *secrets of his heart* (NIV) will be exposed and directed to Christ (verse 25). Such a witness can lead one to sense one's own unworthiness and may very well lead to the worship of God (or conversion).

So what does all this mean? Paul now gives us a brief glimpse into the worship experience of a house church. When they meet together for worship in their individual house churches, every person should make a contribution. But each person's contribution should be for the edification or upbuilding of the fellowship. In this manner, believers support one another—and this is the purpose of the fellowship. If tongues are to be a part of worship, keep the number of speakers to two or three and have someone interpret. If some house churches have no one to interpret, it is better to keep tongues out of the worship ritual. And the same is true of prophecy. Have two or three prophesy to upbuild the others in the fellowship. Those who do not prophesy on a particular occasion can evaluate those who do speak.

If worshipers receive a revelation or insight about something, they are to speak even though they may not have the gift of prophecy (verse 30). In fact, all can give their testimony and then everyone will be encouraged and edified. Furthermore, if one is speaking and does not want to stop and let another speak, the person must be corrected. One prophetic speaker must be subject to another, and in this manner peace is brought to the community rather than confusion. For Paul, the only reason a person should speak in worship is because he or she has a message from God.

Then Paul explains that *women should remain silent* (NIV; verse 34). This instruction does not seem in keeping with what Paul has already said about women in the church (11:3-15). This statement seems very rigid and uncompromising. It is possible that these verses are a later interpretation of Paul, perhaps added by an editor or copier of Paul's letters. It certainly reflects a later time in the church (toward the end of the first century) when there was concern about church practices, morals, lifestyles, and so forth. The *law* to which Paul refers (that subordinates women) is probably the Jewish law. If women wish to ask questions about the faith, they should ask their husbands at home. The advice is directed to the married, but what of the unmarried? Paul concludes with an extreme question (verse 36). Could the gospel have originated with humanity—at Corinth? Is the gospel a human gospel?

A strong case could be made that Paul did not write verses 34-36. However, it is also possible that Paul is facing a particular problem at Corinth. Perhaps a feminist group is abusing the gift of tongue-speaking in some of the house churches at Corinth. In order to address this problem, Paul speaks directly to the situation, possibly explaining the apparent contradictions in his statements.

Paul briefly refers to spiritual gifts in the final verses of this chapter. If a person does not accept Paul's source of authority, then that person is not of Christ and not *recognized* (verse 38, NRSV; NIV= *ignored*). Spiritual and prophetic gifts should be sincerely desired (verse 39; see 1 Thessalonians 5:19-22), but practiced in an orderly or constructive manner.

§ § § § § § §

The Message of 1 Corinthians 14

In the context of agape love, Paul explains that spiritual gifts are real. They are a part of the Christian experience of faith. But spiritual gifts are also primarily for the upbuilding of the community. These gifts must be traded and shared in the life of the believing community. Only in a secondary sense can they be understood as helpful to individual believers. Within this framework, Paul lists faith gifts and orders them according to value.

§ § § § § § §

1 Corinthians 15

Introduction to These Verses

Paul now turns to the central event in the life of Christ.
Apparently some do not believe in the resurrection of the
dead. Paul has gained this information (perhaps again
from Chloe's people) and he wants to put right the
understanding of those in Corinth. Because of Paul's
meeting Jesus on the Damascus road, the resurrected
Christ is a reality close to Paul's experience and deep
faith. This is a topic he addresses clearly,
enthusiastically, and without delay.

The Meaning of the Resurrection (15:1-58)

Paul begins at the beginning. He goes back to his first
preaching and the Corinthians' first hearing of the
gospel. Those at Corinth heard a gospel message that he
first communicated to them. They were deeply moved
and attracted to this message. The message tells of their
salvation, if they *hold firmly* (verse 2). Now Paul again
unfolds the message that he preached.

Paul delivered to them what he received from God.
The message is not Paul's message, interpretation, or
concoction (2:15; Galatians 1:11). God's message to Paul
and to the Corinthians through Paul was that *Christ died
for our sins.* This is in accordance with the only Scriptures
the early Christians had available to them, the Old
Testament. *He* [Christ] *was buried* for human sin. On the
third day *he was raised* from the dead (verse 4). He really
came back to life—and this too was foretold in the Old

Testament Scriptures. This is all proven because he *appeared* to the disciples (especially Cephas, 1:12 and 9:5) alive and well. Here is the essence of Paul's gospel: *died, buried, arisen, appeared.* Following the Old Testament record, God accomplishes everything. God does it all—for humanity.

There is further evidence. Jesus appeared to many more than the disciples. *Five hundred* saw Jesus alive after his death and burial (a possible reference to Pentecost, Acts 1:15 and 2:41). Many of these witnesses are still alive, but some have *died* (NRSV) or are *asleep* (NIV). The use of the word *sleep* as a description for death is adapted by early Christians (John 11:11; 2 Peter 3:4) and is sometimes used to describe the resulting state that follows a violent death. The term describes a sense of peace, freedom, and tranquility. For Paul and the early churches, death itself was not an insurmountable problem. Rather, they focused on Christ and his victory over death, therefore they could use the term sleep.

However, the term can also be misleading. Some have concluded that Paul is referring to a time of separation from God between death (as sleep) and eternal fellowship with the Father through the Son. But based on what Paul writes to the Corinthians in his second epistle (2 Corinthians 5:8), there is no period of absence from God. We could explain Paul's thoughts about death in this manner. When death comes, it appears from the side of humanity that one is asleep. But from the side of God, one goes directly into the presence of the Lord who has won believers for the Father with his death and resurrection.

Then Jesus appeared to *James,* probably referring to Jesus' brother (verse 7; see Galatians 1:19). Paul's reference above to Cephas and the disciples is now expanded to James and *apostles* or missionaries who teach and preach the gospel. Paul seems to exclude himself from this group, indicating that his call to missionary work came directly from Jesus on the Damascus road. Referring to his earlier life with disdain, Paul speaks of himself as one born untimely and not deserving *to be called an apostle*. Then Paul makes reference to his persecutions of Jesus' followers, perhaps an uncomfortable recollection of Stephen's death (Acts 8:1).

Yet the call Paul received is by the grace of God. God does not make mistakes. Even Paul the persecutor was called for God's plan. Paul responded to God's grace and call, becoming a witness and missionary for the kingdom of God arrived and established in Christ.

Now that Paul has created the context or stated the four parts of the gospel, he begins to focus on the resurrection. Paul's manner of thinking is clear: if Christ, then humanity. If Christ's resurrection is the basis of Paul's preaching, how can his preaching be questioned? The resurrection of Christ is a fact, and some Corinthian believers are failing to accept this fact and its clear implications. Then Paul reverses the argument. If there is no resurrection of dead believers, then Christ *has not been raised* (verse 13). If this is true, Paul's preaching and everyone's faith are empty, useless, and meaningless.

Who is the real deceiver if Christ was not raised from the dead? It would have to be Paul and his missionary workers. They are misrepresenting God, because it was God who raised Christ (verse 15). God is behind all this—and Paul is a witness. If dead believers do not share in Christ's resurrection, then neither has Christ been raised. And if Christ is dead, the Corinthian Christians have nothing to believe in and they remain rebellious and distant from God.

It would follow that those *who have fallen asleep* (NIV; NRSV= *have died*) will never be seen again (verse 18). This would also mean that Christ has meaning only for this present life we now live. If this is the case, then Christians should be greatly pitied, because they have placed their trust in any empty and false message. Paul paints a very negative picture. If Christ is not resurrected, the Corinthian believers better look elsewhere for meaning and direction about life and death.

However, this is not the case. Christ's resurrection does not depend upon human beliefs and opinions. The fact is that Christ *has been raised from the dead* (verse 20). He is the first harvest, the one who leads the way, the spearhead that opens the path to life before God. Paul now carefuly states the rationale for his message outlined above. All who have fallen asleep or died will follow him. Through the rebellion of humanity against God (represented by Adam) came death. This death has now been reversed by the new eternal representative of humanity, Jesus Christ. Paul's explanation is complete in its sweeping terms. All are lost in Adam; all are alive in Christ. This is accomplished in an orderly fashion.

Paul's reasoning is logical and Christ-centered. First is Christ the representative of all humanity; then follow those who belong to Christ and are resurrected when he comes; finally, after the rebellion has been defeated, everything is delivered back to God, where it belongs. Paul assures the Corinthian believers that the resurrection has not yet occurred. They have not missed anything. It is the purpose and mission of Christ to bring everything in the creation back to the Creator. The final victory will be over death, which now temporarily rules. When Christ returns, his resurrection will have its full effect on wayward humanity.

Quoting a psalm from the early church's Scripture, Paul explains God's purpose in Christ (verse 27; see Psalm 8:6). In the ordering just noted, Christ is the mediator for God and humanity. For Paul, Christ is God and not a part of the creation. If Christ were of the creation, the gospel would not be from God but from within humanity and within the realm of the creature. Rather, Christ is God the Son, who embraces and takes our humanity fully and completely, redeeming and preserving it forever in the resurrection. When Christ the mediator's crucifixion/resurrection work eventually conquers all for the Father, then the Son will be head of the new Israel *that God may be all in all* (verse 28). For Paul, this resurrection event is the center of the Christian faith. The resurrection is God's purpose for humanity through Christ.

Paul now uses some practical arguments to support his understanding of the resurrection of Christ. His first point seems odd. Paul refers to being baptized *on behalf of the dead* (verse 29). Apparently the Corinth house churches practiced vicarious baptism (or baptism in the place of another). An individual could be baptized in the name of a relative or friend who was already dead. Such a vicarious baptism would have full effect on those already dead. This is an interesting solution first-generation Christians used to bring salvation upon those who died before hearing the Christian message. Whether Paul approves of such baptism is not stated, although by using this argument Paul indicates that he has no difficulty with such a practice.

Now Paul turns to his efforts for the gospel. He is in danger every hour for the sake of preaching the gospel. Yet his pride in the Corinthians is solely because of their foundation in the resurrected Christ. Even if he preached the gospel in Ephesus and had to battle forms of beastly resistance (a confrontation the Corinthians must have known about), is there any gain? *If the dead are not raised* in Christ, then we might as well enjoy a lustful life similar to Jerusalem prior to its destruction by the Babylonians (this is the context of Paul's Old Testament quote, Isaiah 22:13).

Paul concludes these verses with a stern warning. Quoting a Greek proverb attributed to the poet Menander (early 300s B.C.), Paul encourages the Corinthians to stay clear of any who would deny the resurrection of Christ or the resurrection of believers.

Fellowship and company with these persons will corrupt the truth of the gospel. The fact that some do not properly understand and know about the Christian message is an embarrassment to all the members of that house church.

Now that Paul has established the fact of the resurrection, he turns to the nature of the resurrection. Perhaps those who questioned the resurrection did so on the grounds that there could be no practical explanation of a physical body (verse 35). The idea of a spiritual body is not uncommon in Greek thought. But is there a physical body? How will the resurrection of the body occur? What kind of body will people receive?

These are foolish questions, says Paul. Consider such a practical thing as planting a seed. The seed needs to be placed in the ground in order to be transformed into a living plant. Paul's primary emphasis is on transformation, not death. The body of the plant that exists after the transformation is freely assigned by God to each seed. All flesh (and seed) is different, although God has assigned generic consistency and order to the universe. Thus *animals, heavenly bodies, earthly bodies* and so forth will have their own transformed inheritance (verses 39-40). All the heavenly bodies will have their own *glory* (NRSV; NIV= *splendor*).

These events in creation are not unlike what will happen to human persons. An individual will be sown (or planted, buried in the ground) as a mere seed. When the seed is transformed into a plant, it will be imperishable (no longer in need of burial). The seed of our physical body is sown or buried in *dishonor* and rebellion (verse 43); it is transformed to glorify God.

Drawing from the Old Testament (Genesis 2:7), Paul explains how the perishable, dishonorable, weakened physical body of humanity (by way of the first human being) became a seed. The next Adam (Jesus Christ) led the way for transforming the physical body of the first

Adam into the spiritual/physical plant of the resurrection. But the order must not be confused. First comes the seed/body that must be buried or planted in order for the second spiritual/physical body to be harvested. The seed body was fashioned by God from the dust of the earth, from the creation that needs planting. This body is earthly. The second person comes from *heaven* and is of God. Those individuals who live and trust in the dust of the first man are dust; those who live and trust in the heavenly resurrected man Jesus are of heaven and will be resurrected like him (verse 48).

All humanity is born in the image of God. But because of sin, all persons now have the image of rebellious humanity. But when our present seed-state is buried or planted, believers will be resurrected into the image of the resurrected Christ. This new transformed image will be the image of the man in heaven. Paul concludes this profound section with a definition of the kingdom of God. God's kingdom is not of the dust image, but in the image of the resurrected Christ. *Flesh and blood* must be planted and transformed. Only in this manner can humanity be made *imperishable.* For Paul, then, the kingdom of God is defined, based, and established particularly in the resurrection of Christ and generally in the resurrection of humanity.

How is this resurrection going to happen? It is almost as if Paul is raising his voice for a final point. The *mystery* of it all is before us in Christ. Because Christ will return someday, there will obviously be those who will not have fallen asleep (or died). But we should not worry. Those who have not been planted will be instantly changed from a perishable seed to a resurrected spiritual body like Christ. This will happen in a moment, *in the twinkling of an eye* (verse 52), in the shortest possible span of time. The trumpet sound will signal the return of Christ (Matthew 24:31; Revelation 1:10; 4:1) followed by the resurrection of the dead and the immediate change of those still alive.

Paul's explanation suggests that he will be among those yet alive, those to be changed in the twinkling of an eye. About a decade before the end of his life (Paul was probably put to death in the persecutions under Nero, about A.D. 64–65), Paul understands that Christ will return during his lifetime. Paul again quotes from Scripture (Isaiah 25:8; Hosea 13:14), using verses that speak about the end time (verses 54-55).

Now Paul concludes his statements about resurrection and death. Death's finality is caused by sin (see Genesis 2:17). Sin is identified by the law. So Paul's understanding is that rebellion against God (or sin) terminates in death. The law clarifies how we fail to respond to God's love. Christ came on our behalf, being crucified, dead, buried, and resurrected. This is the victory—the only victory—*through our Lord Jesus Christ.* Because he was resurrected, the dead will be resurrected when he returns. So, Paul concludes, do not seek to be strong in yourselves; be strong in Christ. *Excel in the work of the Lord!*

§ § § § § § §

The Message of 1 Corinthians 15

Paul explains in this chapter that the heart of the Christian faith is the resurrected Christ. Because he was resurrected, all will live like him and go directly to be with him after the final baptism of death. For those not asleep, they will be instantly changed. All will be made like the resurrected Christ, receiving spiritual/physical, imperishable, and honorable bodies like Christ.

§ § § § § § §

1 Corinthians 16

Introduction to These Verses

Paul closes his letter in the normal style of the first
century. He opened with gracious greetings. Now he
closes with kindly words. He tells of his travel plans, the
efforts of his helpers, and his concern to raise some
money for those less fortunate in Jerusalem who are
struggling in the midst of a famine.

Update of Collections for the Needy (16:1-4)

The Corinthian believers were already informed about
Paul's collections (Romans 15:25-29; Galatians 2:10). The
believers at Galatia are mentioned, indicating that Paul was
collecting from numerous church communities. The
collection was for the *saints* (NRSV; NIV = *God's people*), or
the believers in Jerusalem. The term *saint* is a description
Paul uses in speaking of believers in general (1:2; Romans
15:26). Based on Paul's statements in this letter, a saint is a
person who lives in Christ. The resurrected Lord is the
saint's wisdom, love, faith, and hope.

What are the Corinthians to do? Paul tells them to put
something aside on the first day of the week. On that
particular day each person is to keep aside a gift offering
for the needy in Jerusalem. In good Jewish tradition, Paul
explains that the amount kept aside should be
determined by the extent to which one prospers. In this
manner, Paul will not have to ask for a special offering
when he comes. He will simply collect what believers
have already put aside before his arrival. When he does

finally manage to visit Corinth, they will together send a reliable person to deliver the offering in Jerusalem. And if they wish Paul to go, the dispatcher will *accompany* Paul.

Travel Plans and Work of Helpers (16:5-18)

Paul tells the Corinthian believers about himself, Timothy, and Apollos. Then he adds some general advice and information.

He talks about his own travel plans to visit the Corinthians after visiting Macedonia. He may *stay* with them, indicating many days or even weeks. If possible, he will stay through *the winter*, meaning several months (verse 6). This would not be an unusual plan, considering that Paul stayed with the Corinthians for several years when he established the community of believers. If Paul will stay with them for the winter, they will help speed him on his journey. That is to say, they will help him determine whether he is to travel to Jerusalem or travel elsewhere.

Paul's relationship with the Corinthians is strong enough for him to wish a stay longer than a few days. He wants to fellowship with them and *spend some time* with them. In this way, he may be able to better help them spiritually. His work is going well at Ephesus, although there are some who are resisting the message of Christ. Paul's plan is to stay in Ephesus until Pentecost, a festival that celebrates God's giving of the law. It is celebrated seven weeks after Passover. This would suggest that Paul is planning to leave Ephesus for Macedonia and then Corinth during the summer months.

Timothy is a faithful helper of Paul. Paul has already referred to Timothy as his beloved and faithful child in the Lord (4:17; see also 1 Timothy 1:2). Timothy is mentioned in Paul's other letters (Romans 16:21; 2 Corinthians 1:1; Philippians 1:1; Colossians 1:1; 1 Thessalonians 1:1; Philemon 1; see also Acts 16:1-3). And Timothy is addressed in two other letters (see 1 and 2 Timothy). Timothy seemed to have a special responsibility assisting Paul in ministry to the

Corinthians (4:17; 2 Corinthians 1:1, 19) and Thessalonians (1 Thessalonians 1:1; 3:2, 6).

Paul's directives to the Corinthian believers suggest that Timothy is young. The house churches are to put him at ease or keep him free from *fear* during his visit, which will apparently occur before Paul visits Corinth. Because Timothy is doing *the work of the Lord*, the Corinthians are to supply his needs during his visit. In this manner, they will *send him on his way in peace* so he can continue helping Paul (verse 11).

Paul also strongly encourages Apollos to visit the Corinthians. Apollos is a converted Jewish believer from Alexandria in Egypt (Acts 18:24–19:1). He is known for his speaking and writing abilities (4:6). His name is mentioned by Paul as a leader of the Corinthian community (1:12). Although Apollos has worked with Paul during Paul's lengthy stay in Corinth, Apollos is not keen to visit Corinth during Paul's absence. Paul attributes this to the will of God.

Paul now interjects a general summary comment about being firm in the faith (verses 13-14). Encouraging the Corinthians to be alert, he directs their attention to the final events that will signal the return of Christ (Mark 13:37; Revelation 3:3). They are to be *firm*, courageous, *strong*, and loving in their faith, recalling the themes Paul has been addressing throughout this letter.

The *household of Stephanas* (verse 15) was the first to embrace the Christian faith in Achaia (the southern part of Greece). Not only were its members converted (this was the only individual whom Paul baptized, 1:16), they also accepted a ministry to the *saints* of the church. In some manner, they were helping believers less fortunate and in need, perhaps supplying food, clothing, and shelter. Paul wants other believers to respect Stephanas and his household's ministry. Respect and subjection are a result of the household's commission: They are called to this work by God and they have been given the means or spiritual equipment to fulfill this calling. Paul is not involved in this commission. It comes directly from God, who opened the eyes of this household to see the need and serve God in addressing this need.

Some members at Corinth traveled to visit with Paul. Stephanas is mentioned; the other two Corinthians are mentioned here and nowhere else in the New Testament. These three individuals have given Paul a taste of true Christian fellowship. This Christian sharing has been a good substitute for his inability to fellowship with the Corinthians. This has *refreshed* Paul, giving him encouragement in his work and ministry. Those at Corinth should give recognition to such men, not because they are mundane workers, but because they are serving God well.

Final Greetings (16:19-24)

Paul, writing from Ephesus, sends greetings from all the Christian fellowships of Asia (see Acts 19:10, 26). He mentions the house church of Aquila and Prisca, who apparently have moved from Rome to Ephesus. Because they had lived in Corinth (see Acts 18:1-2), they would be well known among the Corinthians. The other *brothers* (verse 20) Paul mentions probably refers to those believers in Ephesus who were not members of the fellowship meeting in the household of Aquila and Prisca. Ephesus was similar to Corinth (and all other cities where Christian communities developed), having several house churches associated in a loose fellowship. This loose fellowship encouraged the practice of the *holy kiss*. This ritual was the normal greeting exchanged by believers (Acts 20:37; Romans 16:16; 1 Thessalonians 5:26; 1 Peter 5:14).

Now Paul writes a final greeting. Paul at times dictated a letter to a secretary (see Romans 16:22; Galatians 6:11) and then wrote the final statements himself. His final thoughts include an emphasis on love and Christ's return (verse 22), and a Jewish-type blessing (verses 23-24). Paul's emphasis on love is contrasted with a curse. Because of all that God has done for humanity, and the Corinthians in particular, if anyone chooses not to live in a loving, thankful response to Christ, that person is cursed or separated from God. And almost in an uncontrollable sense of urgency, Paul writes in Greek the phrase *Maranatha,* meaning *Our Lord, come* (see Revelation 22:20). Paul's thoughts are probably running something like this: Hurry, Lord. Do not delay in returning! If you delay, some will choose lifestyles that are not a loving, thankful response to God's grace already completed in Christ.

Paul concludes with a general blessing. This blessing or benediction expresses Paul's basic theology. Because Paul stands with them before God, and because he receives God's grace just as the Corinthians, he now shares out of that love and grace of God, expressing his own concern for their spiritual well-being.

§ § § § § § §

The Message of 1 Corinthians 16

In the body of this letter, Paul has given the Corinthians answers to their questions and offered some key directives of his own. Because he knows the believers at Corinth very well, he can write with affection, energy, and strong encouragement. His close relationship with the believers at Corinth encourages him to share his plans for himself and his workers. This letter gives the Corinthians sound directives to focus their attention on Christ. And just as important, it gives them a sense of how Paul is practically living out the faith he proclaims. His witness is meant to inspire the same in the everyday lives of the Corinthians.

§ § § § § § §

Introduction to 2 Corinthians

As noted in the general introduction, this letter may be a composite of two of Paul's letters. For example, verses 6:14 to 7:1 seem to interrupt the flow of Paul's thought. If these verses were not of the original letter, were they from another Pauline epistle? Or were they written after Paul's death by a member of Paul's circle of workers? Also, chapters 10–13 do not seem to belong to the first nine chapters.

Related to the issue of unity is the sequence of the two Corinthian letters. Twice in this letter Paul refers to an emotional appeal that he previously made (2:4 and 7:12). Could this be the first Corinthian letter? There are some difficulties with this traditional view. First Corinthians is not a tearful letter, nor does it indicate a painful visit by Paul. There seems to be no easy answer that would resolve this issue. Either Paul or Paul's followers (who acted as editors or redactors for this epistle) constructed this letter. Nevertheless, this epistle has entered the New Testament as 2 Corinthians; in this received form, we must examine and consider its message and content.

This letter was probably written during the latter part of A.D. 55. Paul addresses topics touched upon in the first Corinthian epistle. In a more general sense, Paul wants to clarify and explain his apostleship. His purpose is to serve Christ and the gospel. In the same manner, the Corinthian believers are also called to serve Christ and the gospel. This is the overall thrust of Paul's message.

2 Corinthians 1:1-11

Introduction to These Verses

As with 1 Corinthians, Paul opens his second
Corinthian letter in the traditional manner. He gives his
name, the names of those to whom he writes, and he
gives a general blessing. Then he adds an extended
thanksgiving that expresses Paul's deeper theological
perceptions and insights about God, Christ, Paul himself,
and the Corinthian community.

Address and General Blessing (1:1-2)
The letter begins by telling the Corinthian believers
that they are about to hear a letter written by Paul. This
Paul is an *apostle.* Paul understands himself as one who is
sent to the Corinthian people. He is commissioned; he is
personally sent by God to speak a particular message to
Gentiles in general and the Corinthians in particular
(Acts 9:15-16; 15:1-35; Galatians 2:1-10). Paul insists on
this title of *apostle,* even though he was not an eyewitness
of Jesus' earthly ministry (Acts 1:21-26). Paul's insistence
on such an important title can only be explained in the
light of his conversion experience on the Damascus road
(Acts 9) and his sense of calling to the Gentiles.

As in the first epistle, Paul places his calling squarely
in the hands of God. He is an apostle *by the will of God.*
Paul has had nothing to do with this calling. In fact, he
felt he did not deserve such a responsibility because he
had sought to severely persecute the church. But God
does not make mistakes. Paul's message was from God

(1 Corinthians 1:26-31; Galatians 1:11), and his calling is from God. Timothy is mentioned as *our brother*, not having the same apostolic authority as Paul.

Paul refers to the believers at Corinth *as the church of God*. They too, like Paul, have their calling from God. They are a community of believers who have heard the message of Christ. They are a church, an *ecclesia*, a community who make up the body of Christ. Their calling is from God.

Paul places the believers at Corinth with all other believers. With the other Christians of Achaia (the southern part of Greece), they form the body of Christ. In this sense they are *saints* cleansed in Christ and united with the Father through the Son and in the Spirit. They are not morally perfect, but theologically right with God.

Then Paul gives them a blessing. He first mentions God's *grace*, which holds all believers close to God. It is not humanity that finds God; rather, as Paul experienced in his own life, God finds humanity. This grace that holds humanity to God brings *peace*. Peace comes when humanity finds the purpose for which it was created—to be in fellowship with God. Paul explains that this peace comes *from God*. And God is identified as both Father and Son, God's grace and peace come from *our Father and the Lord Jesus Christ*.

Thanksgiving (1:3-11)

In this extended section, Paul gives thanks. He first gives blessings to God, who is *Father*. God was made known to humanity as a father. Before Creation and revelation, God was God. After Creation and revelation, God is Father. The Father of whom? God is first the Father of Jesus Christ, and then the Father of humanity. The Father expresses his character through the Son and in the Son the Father is a God of mercy and comfort. This is the fatherhood of God, the very nature of God.

This God whom we know in Christ comforts humanity (verse 4). Comfort is necessary because rebellion against God causes *affliction* (NRSV; NIV= *troubles*), loss of direction, and confusion. Perhaps Paul is also referring to affliction caused by believers who live out God's values amidst worldly values. Living out the Christian life in the world can often bring persecution and suffering. But God comforts. And the comfort the believer receives from God is not to be kept or hoarded. This comfort is meant to be used for the benefit of the community.

When believers are baptized into Christ, they suffer with Christ (verse 5). As Christ suffered, he pioneered and opened a path back to the Father through the rebellion and sin of the creation. He suffered immensely. Now, as believers follow the pioneer and founder of their faith, they too suffer in the midst of the world's rebellion. In this sense, believers witness to Christ and the work he has completed. And just as Christ suffered and was comforted by the Father, so believers in Christ suffer and are comforted by the Father as brothers and sisters of Christ, the Son.

If Paul and his fellow workers are afflicted, it is for the sake of the Corinthian believers. His concern is to keep them in Christ (*salvation*) and in the comfort of God's grace. When Paul and his fellow workers are comforted, it is the same comfort the believers at Corinth experience—comfort from God. This comfort is experienced *patiently*, by waiting and trusting God to act first (this is a strong Old Testament theme, especially in the Psalms; see Psalms 25 and 27, for example).

Paul's *hope* is for the Corinthian believers to remain before God in Christ. The Father will not turn from them. The final acts of Christ (death, resurrection, and ascension) divinely guarantee the new covenant. If the Corinthian believers remain firm in the midst of the world, they *share* in the sufferings of Paul and his fellow workers. In doing this, they all point to the sufferings of Christ. But then, they also share in God's comfort of humanity that has come back to God in Christ.

This discussion about comfort and affliction leads Paul to speak more personally. Paul and his companions experienced great affliction in Asia. They were very depressed and discouraged (verse 8). They *despaired.* Paul's terminology is very strong and general, perhaps anticipating the particular experiences he later describes (11:22-29; see also Acts 19:23-41). Paul was so overwhelmed by circumstances that he sensed life itself was about to end. But God had a purpose in all this. In the grip of evil circumstances, Paul relinquished everything to the will of God.

Whatever difficulties Paul and his fellow workers experienced, God delivered them. They have learned to depend upon God so that their past deliverance will be repeated. For Paul, this is the essence of the believer's *hope.* In light of these experiences, the Corinthian believers should give continued thanks for answered prayer.

§ § § § § § §

The Message of 2 Corinthians 1:1-11

In these opening verses, Paul directs the attention of the Corinthian believers to God. After identifying himself and the Corinthians as established in God, he explains affliction, suffering, salvation, and comfort as blessings from God. And Paul speaks from experience here. He had sought to proclaim the gospel on his own. In the key verse of this opening section, Paul testifies that he learned through tremendous frustration to rely not on himself *but on God who raises the dead* (verse 9). Paul wants the Corinthian believers to understand themselves by first focusing their attention on God. After this, he turns to their specific problems, needs, and faith experiences.

§ § § § § § §

2 Corinthians 1:12–3:3

Introduction to These Verses

The content of Paul's second Corinthian epistle is
difficult to summarize. (As noted in the Introduction, this
may suggest that 2 Corinthians is a composite letter.) His
thoughts move back and forth from his concern and love
for the Corinthians to Christ's love for the Corinthians. In
this manner, Paul succeeds in giving Christ's sustaining
love for the community at Corinth a very clear personal
accent.

Paul's Concern for the Corinthians (1:12–3:3)

Paul seems to have changed his travel plans. He did not
visit the Corinthian house churches. As he seeks to
explain why, he emphasizes God's plan for him and the
believers at Corinth. The fact that Paul was not able to
visit Corinth does not mean that he is not concerned for
their spiritual well-being. His primary concern is simply
to do the will of God.

Why Did Paul Not Come to Corinth? (1:12–2:4)

Paul begins by asking for understanding. They must
not jump to conclusions. Above all, Paul wants to *boast*
that he has acted with sincerity and responsibility to
God's call and will. God's holy will and God's grace are
the basis of his activity. He does not proclaim the gospel
on the basis of human wisdom. All is from God. And
what he explains here in writing will be understandable

to them. They already know part of his explanation. This may be a reference to the fact that Paul acts in accordance with God's will; or it may refer to partial information that the Corinthians have received. In the end, all will be fully understood when the Lord comes. But for now, just try and understand.

Why, then, did Paul change his plans and not come to Corinth? He had been sure of his plans. He was going to visit them twice, once on the way to Macedonia and once on his way back to Judea or Jerusalem. This would be a double pleasure for them and himself. They could all fellowship together on two occasions. Paul is not attempting to play the Corinthian believers off against himself for some type of personal gain. If a change must be made, it is for God's will. Because all plans and promises *in Christ* are made for the working out of God's will, and because Christ is God's overwhelming eternal Yes to humanity, any changes in human plans are inconsequential. Hence Paul can say *Amen*, meaning *So be it* or *I concur*. The most important plan is God's plan worked out in Christ. This is our irreversible Yes from God.

Behind Christ's work is God (verse 21). God's plan establishes, confirms, positions, or ordains humanity forever. It is God's plan that has commissioned Paul and his workers to proclaim God's Yes to humanity. This they do with God's stamp of approval (*seal*) and by God's Holy Spirit. In light of all this, how can the Corinthian believers be upset that Paul has had to change plans? Those in Corinth cannot question Paul in light of God's Yes and God's eternal plan behind Christ.

However, there is another side to Paul's change of plans. As God is his witness, he wanted to spare those at Corinth discomfort and embarrassment. Paul is not referring to the fact that he and his fellow workers are spiritual guides for those at Corinth. On the contrary, as spiritual guides Paul and his helpers strive for their *joy* and firmness in the faith. But Paul did not want to make *another painful visit* (2:1). During Paul's stay in Ephesus, and following the first Corinthian letter, Paul must have made a quick visit to Corinth. It apparently was a *painful* visit that included confrontations. Paul does not wish to repeat such an experience.

So perhaps his change of plans—from the human side—was good for all involved. Painful confrontations are mutually damaging, helpful to no one, and offer no joy. This is why Paul wrote a letter, to blunt painful and disagreeable confrontations. Paul would rather rejoice in wholesome fellowship with all, suggesting that a small number of believers (or perhaps a house church) were contending with Paul. This tense situation had already encouraged Paul to write a previous letter (see the Introduction; possibly chapters 10–13), which was indeed a tearful and painful epistle. Paul has made all these efforts primarily because he wants them to know how much he loves them and cares for them in Christ.

Paul's Apostolic Commission (2:5–3:3)

Paul seeks to heal the situation at Corinth. Perhaps during his visit or in some other manner an individual has *caused pain* (verse 5). Based on Paul's comments, it is probable that this individual countered or questioned some of Paul's teachings. Thus all have suffered. This person should be censured (*punishment* is really too strong for Paul's Greek term) and corrected by *the majority* (verse 6). But once the person has been rebuked, the community should forgive and embrace him. The community of believers consists of a people called together by forgiveness, sharing a new life based on God's agape love for humanity. This love must be reflected throughout the community. Otherwise, an individual may become spiritually depressed and turn away from the living Christ. Shunning and persecution have no place in the community of believers. Rather,

1 AND 2 CORINTHIANS

believers are called to bear witness to God's love, living in proper response to God's love (see Matthew 18:23-35 for Jesus' teachings).

And now, because the person has been penitent, the problem is over. The Corinthian believers are not to dwell on the difficulty any further. Witnessing to Christ, they must forgive and forget. This is part of the reason Paul is writing to them, to test their response to the situation. Have they been forgiving? Have they been loving? Have they comforted this person? The Corinthian community's acceptance and forgiveness of this person are shared by Paul in the presence *of Christ* (verse 10). With this Christlike attitude of love, the person will not be devastated and *Satan* will not gain a toehold in the community. Satan represents derogatory, manipulative, and conflicting community relationships.

Paul begins digressing, and never finishes the story. Later, in 7:5-16, the account Paul begins here is further developed. Many scholars argue that the section that follows verse 13 (2:14-7:4) belongs to another epistle Paul wrote to the Corinthians. But as noted earlier, we will attempt to understand the structure of 2 Corinthians as the letter stands in the canon of Scripture, being either the work of a redactor (editor) or (less likely) Paul's original structure.

The letter now turns to Paul's preaching of the gospel (verse 12; see Acts 14:27; 1 Corinthians 16:9). *Troas* was a Hellenistic city on the east coast of Asia Minor (present-day Turkey) and just across the Aegean Sea from Achaia and Corinth. Paul's opportunity to preach in Troas is understood as a divine directive and not the result of human luck or good fortune. But even in his proclamation work he is concerned about his brother in Christ and fellow believer, Titus (verse 13). Finding no peace of mind, he crosses the Aegean Sea to the area of Philippi and Thessalonica. Perhaps here in Macedonia Paul receives news about Corinth from Titus.

Suddenly there is a shift in the letter. Paul talks about giving thanks to God. Because of Christ, believers are triumphant over all obstacles that would separate them from the love of God. This victory in Christ seeps into the world like a sweet-smelling *fragrance*. This happens generally because of the Holy Spirit's work, and it happens particularly through the life of every believer. The idea of a sweet fragrance recalls the smell and smoke of sacrifices that were thought in early Jewish tradition to be sweet-smelling to God (Genesis 8:21). For Paul, then, the *fragrance* of God's victory through Christ will go everywhere and become a sweet-smelling response to God. Believers *are the aroma of Christ to God* from among all humanity (verse 15).

By one person, this fragrance is rejected (*death*); by another person, this fragrance is accepted (*life*). No one is adequate for truth in Christ. No one deserves God's grace. God freely chose humanity. Now all are dependent upon Christ. Then Paul beautifully summarizes his call as an apostle. Paul and his fellow workers are not adulterating the gospel by trading or peddling its message for their own advantage. They are first and foremost called by God. Their commission originates from God, and not from humanity. Because of this call, they act in the sight of God and are finally answerable to God alone.

Paul then asks if he is bragging too much (3:1). Perhaps he has been accused of arrogance and self-conceit. Apparently some *peddlers of God's word* (verse 17) came to Corinth with *letters of recommendation*. Paul is not sure whether these letters were addressed to the Corinthian believers or were from the Corinthian believers. Paul and his workers need no such document to prove their authenticity. His letter is the fruit of his labors. The Corinthian believers are living proof of his sincerity and commission from God. Their *hearts* (beliefs) and lives (daily activity) are ample proof of Paul's ministry.

Then Paul reminds the Corinthian believers to live out their testimony to Christ. They should realize their own calling that comes not from a humanly written epistle, but from the very *Spirit of the living God*. The Corinthians—like all believers—are living and moving responses to God. They are not cold mechanical responses, similar to the tablets of commandments in the Old Testament. Paul speaks here of a new covenant, a new loving and living relationship already established in Christ by the loving and living God of the universe.

§ § § § § § §

The Message of 2 Corinthians 1:12–3:3

In this first section of the letter's main message, Paul carefully explains why he has not come to visit the Corinthians. His beginning point is his commission from God. Paul works very hard at explaining how human concerns pale in the light of God's almighty *Yes!* spoken in Christ to all humanity (1:20). As a result of this overwhelming truth, being called by God means one has to be flexible. Paul's change of plans must be understood as God-centered and not as a result of his own personal desires. Paul's sincere concern for the Corinthians stems from this commonality in the gospel of Christ. The most important truth is that the fragrance of the gospel be made known to all. Now Paul can talk more generally about the new covenant that binds them together.

§ § § § § § §

2 Corinthians 3:4-18

Introduction to These Verses

In this section Paul contrasts the old and the new covenants. His distinction centers on the person and work of Christ.

The Old and New Covenants (3:4-18)

The commonality of Paul and the Corinthians is Christ. But what deeper meaning is Paul stating here? Without Christ, Paul and the Corinthians could not have confidence in the character of God. Without Christ, no one would know who God really is. But Christ makes God's character known and understood. Because of Christ, believers can be confident *toward God* (NRSV; NIV = *before God*).

Our gift of salvation is that God is for us. God has established a new and everlasting covenant with humanity. As a result of this covenant, some are called to be ministers. This call includes competence or sufficiency for a greater calling, accomplished continually through the Spirit of the God. The Spirit guides believers to thankfully respond to God for what God has accomplished. This is the new covenant. In contrast, the written code is characterized by legalities, convictions, and guilt. This law kills the spirit of humanity. But the new covenant is founded on Christ and inspired by the Holy Spirit.

Paul now pushes this contrast further between the two covenants (verse 7). The old covenant of the law was

established by the Ten Commandments given to Moses
(Exodus 20:1-17). This is *the ministry* that brought *death.*
The Ten Commandments offer general guidelines for
responding to God's grace expressed in the Exodus,
wilderness wanderings, and giving of the Promised
Land. But because these guidelines cannot be kept, they
condemn. They convict one of what should be done. They
make people guilty. Moses in all his splendor cannot
compare to the glory of the Holy Spirit given in the new
covenant. The new covenant in Christ is permanent and
therefore of far greater splendor.

The new covenant is the Christian *hope* (verse 12). This
hope is not from within humanity. The true hope for the
Corinthian believers is Christ, who has completed and
fulfilled the law for humanity. This Christian hope
should make one very *bold,* because it is God's work and
therefore permanent. The covenant established by God
through Moses lacks this permanence. For Paul, Moses'
veil hid the fading temporary splendor of the old
covenant. Moses' face had shone because he spoke with
God (Exodus 34:29). Because Moses was not God, the
splendor of his face had to fade. By contrast, in the new
covenant Jesus is God. His splendor and glory cannot
fade, but are permanent and forever glorious.

The Jews of the old covenant refused to look beyond
the veil of Moses. Their minds refused to accept God's
new activity in Christ. Now, when the Scriptures are read
(meaning the Old Testament; the New Testament was yet
to be written), the Jews find no indicators pointing to
Christ. When Christ is accepted as God's new act toward
humanity, the veil that conceals the deeper meaning of
the Old Testament is lifted (verse 15; Moses was accepted
as the author of the Torah or Pentateuch). When one
turns to Christ, the veil is lifted and the book comes alive.

How does Paul link together the Holy Spirit and
Christ? This is a complicated question. For Paul, Christ
fulfills the old law on behalf of humanity, living a perfect
life of response to God's initial love. This establishes the
new covenant, freeing humanity for God. But humanity

is not left alone. Christ sends the Spirit of God to humanity (John 14 and 16). The Spirit guides and directs believers to live a life of freedom in thankful response to the Father. Without the work of Christ, the Spirit is not sent. The two are eternally interconnected, yet distinct.

All believers in Christ are *unveiled*. They confront the living Christ as Paul did on the Damascus road, face to face. In this manner, the believers at Corinth behold or better reflect the glory of Christ. Like Moses, they glow and reflect Christ's splendor from daily confronting the risen Lord. The believers at Corinth are being changed bit by bit, degree by degree, into his likeness. They are being changed into the permanence, splendor, and glory of the risen living Christ. How does this happen? In the last sentence Paul again holds together Christ and the Spirit. If one is in Christ, the Spirit is working in him or her, guiding the believer in new-found freedom for God.

§ § § § § § §

The Message of 2 Corinthians 3:4-18

This is a very powerful theological section. Paul contrasts the two covenants, arguing that Christ is the basis of the new covenant. He explains that a believer can be confident about God because of Christ. God has acted toward humanity, sending Christ to do what humanity could not do—fulfill the law. Moses, the law, and the old covenant lack permanent splendor and glory. This first covenant was meant to set the stage for the coming of the new covenant. Hence Christ fulfills the old law (and covenant), giving humanity true freedom for God. Then Christ sends the Spirit to guide and direct believers in using their new freedom in Christ. In this manner, believers are slowly changed into the status of the risen Christ.

§ § § § § § §

PART SIXTEEN

2 Corinthians 4:1–7:4

Introduction to These Verses

Paul now returns to his own ministry and calling. He writes of his faithfulness to the gospel, his hope in Christ, and his continuing work of reconciliation. The emphasis is on God's love and mercy toward Paul. Throughout these verses, Paul is boasting about God's love for humanity made clear in Christ.

Paul, an Ambassador of Christ (4:1–5:21)

Paul begins by explaining that his ministry is only from God. He is called because of God's *mercy* and love. Because it is God's ministry and work, Paul and his fellow workers do not *lose heart.* If the ministry were simply the work of Paul or some human based effort, they would become discouraged. We can almost hear Paul saying that they certainly would have become discouraged if they had to face all the problems of the Corinthian house churches with nothing but their own resources.

How do Paul and his fellow workers practice ministry? In thankfulness to what God's mercy has done for humanity through Christ, Paul and his workers renounce certain ways. If one dies with Christ (Romans 6–8), one is then called to live in full appreciation of Christ. And there must be no tampering with *God's word.* There must be no manipulation of God's word (the Old Testament) for personal gain. Rather, Paul strives for *open* statements *in the sight of God.* Statements open to God have their meaning and source from God and cannot stand alone. They point the believer to God and are not an end in themselves.

In light of such open statements, why have only some hearers come to believe? Paul explains that the gospel is *veiled . . . to those who are perishing* (verse 3). Those who have rejected the good news of Christianity are running from God. To these persons, the gospel is veiled—by their choice and not God's. They have sought worldly gods and want nothing else. They dash away from the *light* of Christ (see 3:13), refusing Christ as *the image of God* or as the truth of God spoken to humanity. But Paul and his workers preach Jesus Christ, not themselves or any other human authority.

Quoting from the Old Testament Creation account (Genesis 1:3), Paul says that God not only spoke, but God's word became action. God said *Let light shine . . .* and the light shone in the darkness. That Creation event anticipated the true and eternal Creation event in Christ. God spoke a word of love to humanity, in the darkness of the human heart. Christ's face shines brighter than the face of Moses and the darkness cannot prevail against Christ the light. As Christ's light shines in our hearts, the true knowledge of God is made known to believers. Paul is saying that in the light of Christ is the truth of God. We know God in Christ and Christ alone.

This truth of God is received in *clay jars* (verse 7). The treasure of God is Christ, the word of God spoken to humanity. This treasure has been deposited with humanity in Christ. This treasure shows that the power belongs to God. It is important to notice that Paul's emphasis is clearly on *treasure, power,* and *God*. The theme is not earthen vessels, even though the verse is often quoted with this emphasis in mind. Now Paul lists the experiences of proclaiming the gospel. And he does this in light of the distinction between earthen vessels and the treasure of God. Earthen vessels may be *afflicted*

[NRSV; NIV= *hard pressed*], *perplexed, persecuted,* and *struck down,* but because of God's treasure in Christ, Paul and his workers are never *crushed, driven to despair, forsaken,* or *destroyed.* The overwhelming power of endurance comes clearly from God.

Paul and his fellow laborers have died in Christ. Because they have died with Christ, they live for Christ. The work they do and the life they live are meant to be witnesses to Christ. In this manner, Jesus is *made visible* to others. Life in the body means constantly dying to Christ, daily and hourly (verse 11). The Christian is meant to be a constant moment-by-moment witness to Jesus Christ. Because of Paul's calling to proclaim the gospel, he must constantly die with Christ. But because he struggles to manifest Christ—especially to the Corinthians—they can grow to maturity in Christ (1 Corinthians 3:1-4). Hence he dies daily; they live.

Like the psalmist in the midst of trouble (Psalm 116:10), Paul and his companions have received the gift of faith. Knowing God and God's truth is to be put right in relation to God and truth. It means testimony, proclamation, and preaching the good news. Hardships are of no consequence. Because Christ was raised, Paul and his fellow workers will be raised; and so will the Corinthian believers. Paul's hardships are for the sake of proclaiming the message of Jesus among the Corinthians. The expected result is that more will hear the message and more will give thanks to God. In this manner, God will receive all the glory.

In the midst of great difficulties, Paul and his companions *do not lose heart* (verse 16). Why? Because he focuses his attention on God, God's treasure given in Christ, and the promise of the resurrection. Because of these truths, the outer nature suffers and deteriorates and the inner person *is being renewed day by day.* And the work is all God's in Christ. Earthly difficulties are referred to as *momentary affliction* (NRSV; NIV= *troubles,* verse 17).

But they are nothing compared to life with God in Christ. They are nothing in the face of the resurrection of Christ. In fact, these temporary difficulties build up a believer's strength in preparation for eternal fellowship with God. These final truths are veiled (verse 18; see 3:12-16). Things seen are for the purpose of the unseen truths of God. The creation is for God's purpose, for the working out of the covenant established by God with humanity.

Referring again to his suffering, Paul calls the earthen vessel an *earthly tent* (5:1). Though the body perishes, all believers *have a building from God.* The true building in the *heavens* is the resurrected Christ. Our earthly body of rebellion and distance from God causes pain and suffering. Because believers have a taste of eternal life in Christ, they *groan* for the *heavenly dwelling,* similar to Israel's groaning in Egypt (Exodus 2:23; see also Psalm 38:8; Romans 8:23). By putting on the heavenly building of Christ, believers are not found rebellious or *naked* before God. Living in the *tent* believers remain anxious. We cannot see clearly (1 Corinthians 13:12). The one hope is the risen Christ, who came in a tent (John 1:14) but has now gone to the Father with our tent. The believer longs to be fully clothed like the heavenly and risen Christ. Death is *swallowed up by life,* the life of Christ. God prepares and accomplishes this work in believers through the Holy Spirit. The work is God's, from beginning to end.

With this truth in mind, Paul suggests that the believer be *confident* (verse 6). The risen Lord is with the Father and the believer is in the temporary home/tent of the body. The believer lives by *faith* in the risen Christ. Because Christ is with the Father and at a distance from the believer, the Christian cannot walk by sight. But faith in Christ includes courage and confidence because Christ is with the Father on behalf of all believers. Paul and his fellows are courageous and confident in the face of tremendous odds. Nevertheless, they would prefer to be with the Lord (Philippians 1:21) and established in the newness of Christ's resurrection. Paul is indicating here that his death will now probably come before Christ's return, and that following death one goes directly to be with the Lord (see his earlier thought in 1 Corinthians 15 where the dead *sleep,* waiting for the Lord to return).

Regardless of whether Paul and his workers find themselves in heaven (*home*) or on earth, their primary task is to *please* the Lord (verse 9). God freely chose humanity for fellowship; now a person's task is to be thankfully responsive and obedient to God. Persons will be judged on the basis of their response to the good news of the gospel. This judgment will occur through Christ, who died for all. So all must prepare accordingly.

Because Paul and his companions know *the fear of the Lord,* they strive to present the gospel to all. The fear of which Paul speaks carries the double meaning of thankfulness (reverence) to God and the anxiety of falling away from God. Then Paul adds that the most important point is not that he and his workers know God, but that God knows him and his fellow workers. This should be obvious to those at Corinth. Paul is not bragging. There were apparently some among the Corinthian house churches who respected position rather than sincerity. Paul suggests the believers at Corinth can be proud of him and his workers because they rely only on Christ and God's grace.

If Paul and his helpers seem too enthusiastic or ecstatic, it is due to God's grace. His moods of spiritual ecstasy are from God. His moods of rational argument also stem from God. Whatever he does, it is for their spiritual benefit. But really, moods are unimportant. What is important is the permanent unchanging truth of God behind their moods. God's power is God's truth in Christ. Christ expresses the love (*agape*) of God. He died and was raised again in order to reconcile all humanity to God. Now the task is to get the message out to all who will listen, so that individuals will live for Christ and not for themselves.

Paul and his fellow workers do not understand people as mere human beings. Persons are understood as coming from God. Offering an early view of Christ, Paul explains that some viewed Christ as merely a human person. But eventually—after the Resurrection—Jesus was understood as God who had become man. As Christ is, so is humanity. Then Paul adds a marvelous verse explaining how every human being must now be perceived (verse 17). Seen from the perspective of God in Christ, everyone is a new creature, a new creation. Why? Because everyone is reconciled to the Father through the Son. This statement by Paul only makes sense when understood from the perspective of God's love and grace expressed toward humanity once and forever in Christ. The work of the Son makes the old rebellious nature pass away. In Christ, the new humanity has come through his death and resurrection.

Again Paul emphasizes how he understands all this. *All this is from God* . . . (verse 18), who heals the broken and fractured relationship between God and humanity. Now persons who have experienced this grace are called to pass the word and proclaim the message to others. The message of those who proclaim the gospel is clear. In the life and work of Christ, God was *reconciling the world to himself* (verse 19). This is the message that Paul and his fellow workers must proclaim. God acted. And there are no strings attached. All is accounted for.

The status of Paul and his fellow workers is that of *ambassadors for Christ* (verse 20). Based on what has just been said, this does not imply status or a position of privilege. God alone has done the work. It is completed in Christ. An ambassador's task is not an easy one, and Paul is not priding himself in this calling. God simply makes the appeal through those like Paul who are called to proclaim the gospel. Paul summarizes his proclamation as an ambassador with the appeal *to be reconciled to God*. Reconciliation is completed by God through Christ. Christ was without sin. But he took our humanity, and in doing so his perfection accepted the responsibility and result of human rebellion. This caused him to suffer and die on the cross. He was made *to be sin who knew no sin*. Because he then healed the broken relationship between God and humanity, now those who believe in him *become the righteousness of God*—by God's doing in Christ and not by any effort of humanity. For Paul, all the hardships and suffering he experienced were a small price to pay for the excitement of proclaiming such a glorious gospel.

Paul's Love of the Corinthians in Christ (6:1-13)

Because Paul's preaching has present and future significance, he appeals to the believers at Corinth. As an ambassador, Paul is working together with Christ (6:1). Because of Christ's death, resurrection, and ascension, God's grace is completed and sure. They are loved and accepted, reconciled by God in Christ. If they do not respond to God's grace, they are vain or empty in the face of the gospel. Quoting the prophet Isaiah (49:8), Paul encourages the Corinthian believers to respond in the present time. Salvation has arrived. The Old Testament prophecy is true now. The end is not far away. They are now in the interim period when God waits for people to accept the offer of reconciliation. Paul asks that they not keep God waiting.

Paul gives them nothing but Christ. Any other message beyond Christ becomes an obstacle to reconciliation. Paul's ministry points and refers people to Christ. There is no other truth. In this manner, Paul's ministry is faultless. Then Paul surprisingly commends himself and his fellow workers to the Corinthians (verse 4). What Paul means by *commend* is not pride to work well done. For Paul, only Christ has done a perfect and complete work. Rather, Paul uses the word *commend* because of hardships. His great *endurance* and many painful experiences commend his sincerity and concern to the Corinthians. At the same time, his ministry includes many signs that are evident blessings from God. And God's *righteousness* in Christ keeps him fully equipped for every situation, *for the right hand and for the left* (see also 10:4; Romans 6:13; 13:12).

Then Paul identifies a series of attitudes toward himself and his fellow workers. We can assume that these are reputations the early evangelists experienced. Paul contrasts good and bad attitudes toward himself and his helpers. Sometimes they are accepted as speaking the truth; at other times they are accused of proclaiming lies and statements of deceit. These reputations indicate acceptance or rejection of the gospel. Jesus clearly stated to his followers that they would be persecuted for his sake and for the sake of the gospel (Matthew 10:1-42). The gospel message cuts across worldly values and either changes the one who hears or causes rejection and further rebellion. It is this contrast that lies at the heart of Paul's statements.

In all Paul's suffering and persecution for the gospel, he is not bitter (verse 10). His fellowship with God in Christ through the Holy Spirit far surpasses any inconvenience he experiences. He may be sad, but in his heart he is *always rejoicing*. As an apostle of Jesus the Christ, he may appear poor, but being reconciled to God he is truly rich in eternal things. The believer may appear to be desolate; but in reality, the person in Christ has *everything* that holds eternal value.

Then Paul makes a final appeal to the Corinthians. He explains that he has been talking very freely, literally with an open mouth. He has held nothing back. His heart has been laid bare. He has kept no secrets from them. In this openness and freedom between himself and the Corinthian believers, there are no legal requirements or

1 AND 2 CORINTHIANS

restrictions. The Corinthians are not cramped for space in their relationship with Paul. This relationship is based primarily on the gospel of Christ. In this gospel, Paul places no restrictions on them except that they rely solely upon Christ. However, they will feel affection for Paul because he brought them the gospel. These genuine affections may restrict them in what they would say and do in response to Paul's directives. Speaking without apostolic authority, Paul requests that his spiritual *children* be honest and truthful with Paul and his workers.

The Corinthians Must Cling to Christ (6:14–7:4)

These verses seem to intrude on Paul's train of thought. This section could have been inserted for one of two reasons: Either these verses comprise a section from another Paul-to-Corinth letter, or they are an explanation inserted by one of Paul's fellow workers after Paul wrote the letter. But the exact transmission and evolution of this letter are not known. It was probably edited in some manner based on the historical situation among the house churches in Corinth.

These verses encourage the Corinthians to remain strong in Christ. The secondary theme is the Corinthians' relations with pagans or unbelievers. Speaking in Jewish metaphors, Paul warns that the believers at Corinth must not dilute their faith in Christ (verse 14). *Partnership* and *fellowship* imply close relations, almost in a legal sense. If believers associate closely with non-believers, the result may be compromise or half-hearted commitment to Christ. Paul then asks more directly, What harmony is there between Christ and the devil? The word *Belial* or *Beliar* appears in the first and second centuries B.C. as a Greek term for Satan, or the prince of evil (in the Greek Old Testament this term is used to translate *evil* in Judges 20:13). The *believer* is one who has put his or her trust in God. For the believer, everything now comes from God.

Because this is not true and not understandable for the unbeliever, how can they have anything in common?

The same type of rhetorical question is again asked, emphasizing the *temple of God* (verse 16). In the Old Testament, the Temple was the place where God lived. In Paul's theology, the temple has two interrelated meanings: On the one hand, *temple* refers to all the house churches of Corinth (1 Corinthians 3:16); on the other hand, *temple* refers to every individual believer (1 Corinthians 6:19). In either sense, the temple can have nothing to do with idols. Loosely quoting several Old Testament verses, Paul offers substance to what he has been saying. Paul has been speaking, but God has spoken and acted in the past. God has promised to live in believers (Leviticus 26:12; see also Isaiah 53:4; Ezekiel 37:27), God's people will be holy and separate (Isaiah 52:11; see Jeremiah 51:45), and God will be their Father (2 Samuel 7:14; Ezekiel 20:34). These are powerful themes found throughout the Old Testament and strongly embedded in Jewish theology. They are a good summary of the previous verses, placing all the emphasis on God's love and action. The Corinthian believers should understand their lives from God's perspective and not from a human perspective.

Then Paul adds a powerful statement of purpose (7:1). Because God's promises are the basis of the Christian life, believers can enthusiastically respond to God. Everything begins with God. God acts first. But because God acts, Paul suggests that the believers in Corinth *cleanse* themselves. The cleansing is not so God will save them. God has already saved them in Christ through the Holy Spirit. Self-cleansing is appreciation for what God has accomplished. Bodies and spirits should be presented to God *as a living sacrifice, holy and acceptable* [NRSV; NIV= *pleasing*] *to God* (Romans 12:1) in response to what God has done. In this living response to God, the believer is not merely taking *holiness* for granted, but is living out that holiness in thankful respect (*fear*) of the Lord.

In the final three verses of this section, Paul encourages the Corinthians to respond sincerely to God. Although rumors may abound, Paul and his workers have taken advantage of no one. Because the Corinthians are in Paul's heart, they should take him into their hearts too. Paul is not negative or condemning. He is not being critical out of personal vengeance. He loves them in Christ, and together they live and die in Christ.

§ § § § § § §

The Message of 2 Corinthians 4:1–7:4

Throughout this section Paul concentrates on his ministry and message. His apostolic ministry is open to God in that he and his fellow workers struggle to present Christ. They are ambassadors for Christ and not individuals of authority and prestige. Their ministry begins with Christ and ends with Christ. Even though they experience hardships, pain, and suffering, they are happy, joyous, and unperturbed. And like Paul, the Corinthian believers should grow and strengthen inwardly and decline outwardly. This hope is in Christ, who establishes them as a new creation through reconciliation.

There is one outstanding feature that Paul emphasizes throughout this section. Perhaps it is a result of Paul's need to defend his apostleship in the midst of some house churches. But Paul's main emphasis is that God acts first. God first called Paul, God now sustains Paul and his fellow workers, and God makes promises to all believers. Paul's apostleship is a response to God's act of reconciliation. And all those in Corinth are also called to live in response to God's reconciliation.

§ § § § § § §

Introduction to These Verses

Paul now turns to three themes that extend his proclamation of God's reconciling work in Christ. The previous section emphasized his own experiences and apostleship. He reflected on his past and related his experiences to the Corinthian believers. Paul again begins with action—but this time human action that follows the action of God. The action Paul speaks of in this section is future action, but again it is a future action based upon God's action in Christ.

Paul Rejoices in News of the Corinthians (7:5-16)

Paul again mentions his trip to Macedonia in northern Greece. He apparently had to face those who opposed him and his gospel. At the same time, he is concerned about the long-overdue Titus, who is to bring him word from Corinth. Amidst all his problems and difficulties, Paul is eventually comforted by Titus's safe arrival. The implications are that Paul has been deep in prayer for Titus. With Titus's arrival, God answers Paul's prayer, allowing Paul to see beyond his immediate circumstances and be comforted by God's grace. Of equal joy is the news that Titus brings from Corinth. He too has been comforted in learning of the fairly good state of the Corinthian house churches. Paul is comforted for several reasons. He is delighted to learn of their desire to have him visit; he is pleased to learn that they are sad because he has chosen to stay away; and he rejoices to learn that they are not lukewarm toward Paul but accept his leadership with *zeal* (NRSV; NIV= *ardent concern*).

Being absent from the situation in Corinth, Paul is uncertain how his letter will be accepted. Somewhat embarrassed, he apologizes for hurting them. He has regretted writing the letter, but he feels no longer angry because the epistle was painful only momentarily and has now accomplished growth and maturity in Christ. Which letter Paul is writing about here is uncertain. Some scholars have argued that Paul is referring to 1 Corinthians. Others have argued that *my letter* refers to either a portion of 2 Corinthians or a letter now lost.

In any case, now Paul rejoices (verse 9). As usual with Paul, his rejoicing is in God. The Corinthians' *grief* (NRSV; NIV= *sorrow*) refers to their sense of guilt before God. They see their actions as God sees their actions. Because Paul's letter directs them to God, they suddenly realize that they are straying from God's will. As a result, the letter creates no tense relations between Paul and the Corinthians. Paul then contrasts *godly grief* and *worldly grief* (verse 10). Godly grief directs a person to see himself or herself in relation to God. In the face of such hopeless circumstances before God, a person is thrown upon God and God's mercy. Godly grief leads to *repentance* and *salvation*. Worldly grief creates a guilt that throws a person back upon his or her own personal resources. This grief includes hatred, resentment, and anger, and in the end brings *death*. For Paul, then, sin is most obvious when a person first looks to God, and not first to the self or to the world. Looking first to the self and the world simply causes more distortion.

The Corinthians are an example of what godly grief produces. By looking to God in order to clearly see sin and errors of living, the Corinthian believers have fallen back upon Christ alone. Now they are taking the matter very seriously—in Christ. They are keen to defend Paul and punish or discipline the person who attacked Paul's ministry and apostleship. The problem was not caused by the community as a whole. Generally, the community had clung to Christ and its members were *innocent* [NIV; NRSV= *guiltless*] *in the matter*. So Paul is pleased he wrote the letter. He is not finally pleased because a person's wrong was exposed or even because the one who suffered the wrong was comforted, although these are commendable developments. But Paul is finally pleased because the Corinthian believers' care and love for him are made known to themselves and to God. The painful letter brought them to their senses. They hold Paul in great affection; this is part of their thankful response to God for the good news of Christ.

Throughout this letter the meaning behind Paul's use of Greek pronouns is not always clear. In this present section, this is especially a problem. Is Paul referring to himself and his fellow workers when he uses the pronoun *we,* or is this just a figure of speech that designates only himself? (Certainly some of his fellow workers were not acquainted with the Corinthian believers.) When Paul refers to himself, does the pronoun he uses include his fellow workers? Although this confusion does not really change the meaning of the letter, it is worth noting.

Now Paul returns to the news brought by Titus (verse 13), Paul is *comforted* (NRSV; NIV= *encouraged*) about all this and he is delighted that Titus is pleased. Titus had clearly been impressed with the general situation at Corinth. He was encouraged that they had responded to Paul's directives. Prior to Titus's visit, Paul had boasted about the Corinthian community of faith. Paul was not proved wrong.

Paul then connects the gospel he preached among the Corinthians with their present sureness in Christ. He explains that their current life in Christ attests to the gospel Paul proclaims. Titus is deeply moved because of the Corinthian believers' obedience to the gospel. Titus also deeply appreciated their acceptance of his visit, a visit that may have had as its primary purpose the gathering of a collection for the poor in Jerusalem (8:6). Paul now rejoices because he has *complete confidence* in the Corinthians. Paul's confidence is not in the Corinthians' own strength and spiritual muscle. Rather, his confidence is based on Titus's testimony that those in Corinth are squarely grounded upon Christ and so are reconciled to God.

Collection for the Jerusalem Believers (8:1–9:15)

Paul now writes with enthusiasm about his project to help the poor in Jerusalem. There were some problems with care for the poor in Jerusalem earlier (Acts 6:1-6), suggesting that believers in Jerusalem were from the poorer classes (and this may have been complicated by a famine). Paul had already mentioned the collection in his first Corinthian epistle (1 Corinthians 16:1-4), even suggesting a method for collections, following the Jewish idea of almsgiving. Titus had just returned from Corinth, apparently working on the collection project. Now Paul gives considerable space to explaining his work. Paul probably reckons that his current good relations with the Corinthian house churches present an ideal time for emphasizing his project.

The church communities in Macedonia were generous and gracious in their giving. Paul is referring at the least to believers in Philippi, Thessalonica, and Berea (Acts 17:10). From the start, Paul attributes their generosity to *the grace of God.* They are giving in thankful response to the gospel of Christ. Paul states that they were afflicted in some manner. Perhaps the affliction was their *extreme poverty,* even though Macedonia was a rather prosperous area of the Roman Empire. Perhaps they were experiencing a regional famine. Or the Christian communities may have been persecuted by other more widely accepted religious movements. In spite of the Macedonians' poverty and affliction, their generosity overflowed. They gave freely beyond their means (verse 3), being keen to take part in this project of supporting the *saints* or the poor in Jerusalem.

The Macedonians made their giving a general act of devotion. Here is an order for Christian giving. First a believer responds worshipfully to God because of God's grace that has reconciled humanity. Second, the Macedonians respected the particular apostle God had commissioned to preach the gospel in their midst. By respecting Paul they further expressed thankful worship to God. Finally, they gave generously as further appreciation and thankful worship to God. Because of the Macedonians' contributions to the collections, Titus was asked to involve the Corinthians in the offering. As the cup of the Corinthians overflows in spiritual gifts—belief, insightful knowledge, keenness, speaking in tongues, and so forth—they should make an effort to support the poor in Jerusalem as well with material gifts to the best of their ability.

Paul does not want the Corinthian believers to think he is demanding and commanding that they do something. Nothing is demanded by Paul. He respects their independence and foundation in Christ. Paul then makes a healthy comparison between the Corinthians and the Macedonians. If the Corinthians support the collection, their deeds will clearly indicate that their love is *genuine* (NRSV; NIV= *sincere*) like the love of the Macedonians. The only example for such agape love is Jesus Christ. Here Paul gives a mini-summary of the gospel. Christ was *rich*, at one with the Father in perfect fellowship before Creation. This richness Christ gave up, becoming *poor* in order to rescue humanity and reconcile all to God. This is God's *grace* offered in Christ that the Corinthians *know* so well. And this is how they have *become rich* (see Romans 15:3; Philippians 2:7).

Paul is offering the Corinthians practical advice based on theological truths. The Corinthians had already been enlisted to support the poor in Jerusalem in the previous calendar year (1 Corinthians 16:1-4), even before the Macedonians had become involved. Now they should carry through their pledged support. They had been willing to do this work; now they should bring it to completion to the best of their ability. As they are willing, they will be judged only on the basis of what

1 AND 2 CORINTHIANS

they have and what they can give. They are not meant to give more than they can afford; otherwise they would become poor and those in Jerusalem would be comfortable. Rather, Paul simply means that their comfort can be used to help support the needs of the poor in Jerusalem. This concern for equality is an attempt to strike a balance of means among believers. Paul then quotes the Old Testament (Exodus 16:18), reinforcing his statements. His quote comes from passages describing the wilderness wanderings when Israel was dependent upon God for each day's food.

Titus had been keen to help with the collection in the past. It is interesting that Paul's *thanks* are to God and not to Titus. God is the initiator of the good news, the sender of the Holy Spirit. It is God's grace that is behind Paul's concern for the Corinthians. It is also God's grace that inspires Titus's *concern* (NIV; NRSV= *eagerness*) for the Corinthians. Titus's heart is so moved that he zealously volunteers himself. He visits the Corinthians as a result of Paul's request for help. Titus is to be sent with a fellow believer. This unnamed brother is a famous preacher or speaker among *all the churches* (verse 18). He has been appointed for elected by the churches of Macedonia and Philippi. His appointment was to travel first for the glory of the Lord and secondly for Paul's and his companion's good will toward the Corinthian believers.

Paul understands that such work carries potential danger. He and his workers could be accused of misusing the funds for their own advantage and enjoyment. But Paul knows they are to be responsible, first before God and then before humanity. Irresponsibility is harmful and destructive to the gospel. It is the opposite of witnessing to the gospel's truth. Then Paul mentions a third person who will travel to Corinth. This person comes directly from Paul's group of workers, suggesting that the brother previously mentioned (verse 18) may have come from Macedonia or Philippi. This third individual is well-known to Paul and a proven worker for the gospel, *eager in many matters* (NRSV; NIV=*zealous*) through the Holy Spirit. Titus is given high status among Paul's fellow workers. The others too are *messengers* (NRSV; NIV= *representatives*), or literally apostles, *of the churches*. Together they constitute a group whose primary purpose is to glorify Christ. Now it is up to the Corinthian believers to offer practical proof of what this three-man team has been told about their love and kindness.

Paul now turns to the meaning of the collection. He has dealt with those who will see this work through. But what does it all mean? It means serving God by helping fellow believers or *saints* (9:1). And the Corinthians know this. So Paul should not have to continue explaining himself. Paul knows they are willing to help. Those in Macedonia know because Paul has told them. The people of Achaia (the lower part of Greece where Corinth was a major Christian center) had been so enthusiastic that they encouraged the Macedonians. So it is time to act and not simply talk about sending help to the poor in Jerusalem. Not acting now when they are ready leaves open the possibility that they will not be able to act later due to unforeseen circumstances. Then everyone would be embarrassed. So Paul has sent *the brothers* on ahead (verse 5). The time is right. Delays must be avoided so that the promised gift remains a gift rather than a requirement.

Paul turns to the generosity of the Corinthian believers. The word of God that is sown in the heart *sparingly* means that the spiritual blessings received will be similar. And of course the opposite is also true. Each believer should respond to God's grace in Christ as led by the Holy Spirit. Such a response to God should be done with joy. Paul suggests that living in response to God's grace can be done with a smile or a frown. God receives much more appreciation when we give thanks joyfully. When God's word spoken in Christ is fully planted in the heart, there is no limit to the blessings of those who live only in response to God's truth—the righteous of God.

Now Paul makes a marvelous statement about serving God. God's word spoken in Christ is the *seed* supplied to the sower (verse 10). The sower is first the Holy Spirit and secondly Paul and his fellow workers. God supplies complete reconciliation and a full ration for all daily needs. If one is led to help supply the needs of others, God will make the harvest plentiful for all. But for Paul, believers receive everything from God; believers are then meant to give everything back to God in thankful response. The Corinthians' generosity as thanksgiving to God will be channeled through Paul and his workers because of their responsibility for the collection and distribution of the offering for the poor. There are two advantages: First, the poor are helped in Jerusalem, where the faith historically originated. Second, their generosity will express many thanksgivings to God (verse 12).

By offering help to the saints in Jerusalem, they will be serving God. Their service will be a glorifying response to God, bearing witness to the gospel of reconciliation. Their *obedience* expressed as *generosity* will offer worshipful thanks to God for Christ's completed work. This will stand as their living confession, their clear witness to God's grace, throwing those in Jerusalem and elsewhere back upon God and God's ever-present grace. Their action will point persons to God. This observation allows Paul to conclude his theme by giving thanks to God and not to the Corinthians. Because of God's *indescribable gift* in Christ, the Corinthians now give in thankful response. *Thanks be to God!*

§ § § § § § §

The Message of 2 Corinthians 7:5–9:15

In this section, Paul deals with the ever-present problems of Christian charity. But throughout, Paul consistently chooses to deal with giving only in a theological manner. As a result, giving by believers is not the primary characteristic of a Christian. The primary characteristic—the only characteristic—of a Christian is Christ. Because the Father gave his Son for the reconciliation of humanity, Christian charity and giving are always a response to God. In this way, giving can never become a reason for God loving a believer. Generous giving can only be an obedient, worshipful, and thankful response to God. Thus, in all Christian charity, God is the primary actor. Giving bears witness to God's eternal giving. And Paul refuses to consider charity and Christian giving in any other manner.

§ § § § § § §

2 Corinthians 10:1–12:13

Introduction to These Verses

There is a clear break in the epistle at this point. These verses indicate a different theme. They leave the plans for an offering and turn to Paul's apostolic work. Paul now begins speaking about himself as "I" and "me" rather than "we." But the most noticeable change in this section is the general circumstances at Corinth. Suddenly there seem to be questions and doubts concerning Paul's apostleship. This type of personal appeal by Paul is not unusual in his letters (Galatians 5:1-12; Ephesians 3:1-19; Philemon 19), but such a topic following his encouragement that the Corinthians support the collections for the poor seems out of place. Suddenly the mood is one of distrust rather than encouragement. This has prompted many scholars to argue that chapters 10–13 comprise a different letter. Nevertheless, these chapters will be treated as part of the letter's total content and message.

Paul Boasts of Laboring in the Lord (10:1-18)

Paul begins with great forcefulness (verse 1). He strongly urges the Corinthian believers, beginning with their motivation. He does not first identify the goal he wishes to urge them toward. Rather, he wants them to be encouraged spiritually by Christ's characteristics. These traits of Christ refer to his *meekness and gentleness* in coming down to earth from heaven for the work of reconciliation (Philippians 2:6-11; see also 2 Corinthians

8:9). Paul is being bold in his directive here. When he is in their presence he is *humble* (NRSV; NIV= *timid*), not wishing to cause tension and confrontation. However, in letters he can say things more bluntly. Paul is hopeful that when he comes he will not have to display boldness to all in Corinth. But he will have to show confidence to some who think he is acting according to worldly *standards*. And some think that Paul is acting for personal gain and advancement.

Paul acknowledges that all believers *live in the world* (verse 3; NIV; NRSV= *as human beings*). Although believers are in the flesh, they are not of this world. Their citizenship is the kingdom of God or the kingdom of heaven. Believers have no part in an earthly war. Christians certainly do not rely on worldly weapons, human strengths, and earthly powers. Paul's gospel is from God. *Arguments* are useless in the face of this gospel. Every human thought is brought to the truth of God in Christ. Wrong responses to the gospel are *disobedience* and human rebellion (verse 6). When the Corinthian believers hold firmly to the gospel, those who invade Paul's mission field in Corinth will be shown to be disobedient and will bring punishment upon themselves.

Paul begins a very complicated section by telling the Corinthians to ponder their present situation (verse 7). For those who are well-established in Christ—and only those persons—their situation is the same as Paul and his fellow workers. They are all Christians. Christ is the basis and meaning of their existence. Because of this solid foundation in Christ, Paul has boasted of his position and leadership. But his very *authority* has a purpose, that of building up and strengthening the believers at Corinth. Paul's authority is not for their disadvantage. Therefore, he has been zealous to their advantage. For this reason, those who criticize him are wrong. Paul should not be ashamed. But in order to help the situation, Paul will not claim divine authority for fear of *frightening* them.

Now Paul provides an indication of what intruding

missionaries have said about him (verse 10). His letters (coming from a distance) are difficult to understand, his physical presence is not impressive, and his speech (phraseology and content) is not commanding. Why should the Corinthians think he is a great leader? To these accusations Paul responds without delay. First of all, there is no inconsistency in what Paul says in their presence and what he writes in his letters. If those in Christ carefully consider Paul's teachings, speeches, and letters, they will realize that these claims are absolutely false. Christ is consistently the content of Paul's message. Second, Paul wants no comparisons between himself and these other self-proclaimed leaders. His only foundation is Christ, and not human comparisons.

Paul and his workers do not *boast* in what others have done. Unlike those who are causing trouble among the Corinthians, Paul does not claim the work of others. Rather, Paul wishes to keep the house churches in Corinth centered on Christ, trusting in his work of reconciliation. As these Corinthian believers mature in their faith, Paul is hopeful that others living in their city will come to believe. In this manner, Paul will be able to preach through the Corinthians, bringing the gospel message to a greater and greater number of people. Paul's boasting will only be in Christ. He will not have to rely, like these other foreign missionaries, upon the work of others. As Paul wrote to the Corinthians once before (1 Corinthians 1:31), the only boasting to do is in the Lord (verse 17). Paul summarizes what he has been saying in a beautiful statement. The authority that is eventually accepted is the person who acts and leads because of God's appointment. A human appointment is empty, especially a self-asserted commendation.

Paul Is a Fool for Christ (11:1–12:13)

In this section, Paul is responding to criticism that has been directed against him. It seems apparent that the criticism is coming from the person or persons mentioned in the section above. But Paul is unrelenting. He will not allow his focus to be directed away from Christ. Whether in boasting or in weakness, Paul's only claim throughout these final paragraphs is God's resurrected Son who has reconciled the creation to the Creator.

Now Paul is going to indulge in a little extravagant thinking, based on God's action in Christ. The Corinthian believers should try and follow his foolish thoughts (and so he encourages them throughout; 11:16, 17, 19, 21; 12:6, 11). This is the only way they will be encouraged to see the truth. Paul is keen to have them be strong in the Christian faith. But Paul's *jealousy* is not his own. He senses God's jealousy, wanting the Corinthians to seek only God's will. The word *jealousy* seems to trigger in Paul's mind the imagery of marriage. He explains God's divine *jealousy* as the result of marrying the virgin Corinthians to the one husband of Christ.

Continuing the analogy, Paul points out that Eve, the bride of Adam, was deceived in the garden of Eden. In a few strokes of the pen, Paul aligns the intruders at Corinth with the serpent (Genesis 3) and the believers at Corinth with Eve, the bride of Adam. Paul is sincerely concerned that the Corinthians may well be deceived and distracted from the resurrected and living Christ. If they allow others to present them with *another Jesus, a different spirit, or a different gospel,* then they are accepting error.

What does this verse tell us about the situation in Corinth? On the one hand, by allowing these other missionaries to speak about *another* godly truth, the people of Corinth are tolerating and therefore accepting such ideas. The Corinthians should not even give such alternate views a hearing. They have the truth in Christ. On the other hand, we get a picture here of what the troublemakers in Corinth were proclaiming. (1) They were professing a different Jesus from the resurrected living Jesus Christ that Paul proclaimed. The use of the term *Jesus* suggests that they perhaps were teaching an earthly Jesus who was not fully God. (2) They emphasized a different *spirit*. Perhaps they focused their attention on the human spirit and called this spirit divine. (3) They taught a different gospel, one that perhaps included human effort and good works in exchange for reconciliation.

From the very early days of Christianity, there were variations and different interpretations of the Christian faith. These shades of meaning caused early rivalries. Extreme differences were eventually overcome in the fourth and fifth centuries by general church councils that generated statements of faith (Nicea, Chalcedon, and so forth). During the Reformation (1500s), church authority was replaced by biblical authority, opening the way once again for various interpretations of Jesus the Christ. In this sense, the Christian faith today is very similar to the Christian faith in the first century, especially in Corinth.

Paul then calls them *apostles* (verse 5). In fact, he refers to them as *super* (*superlative*) apostles. Paul ironically refers to their teachings and claims that apparently exceeded Paul's teaching and claims. But Paul refuses to be intimidated. His inability to speak well and dynamically (10:10) is a shortcoming, but the knowledge that he has received from Christ is great. Paul's knowledge through Christ has been made clear in that he has addressed all their problems and has offered sound theological teachings for every situation.

Although Paul could have expected material and financial support from the Corinthians (1 Corinthians 9:4-18), he received no such support. Should he be seen as less in their eyes? Paul's only concern was to bring the gospel to the Corinthians. He did not see this work as his way of making a living. Furthermore, by not receiving money and other support he did not distract from the gospel of Jesus Christ. Yet he did receive missionary support from other churches. Even though he pursued his trade in Corinth (Acts 18:3), he did not make his needs known to the Corinthians when provisions were low. Rather, he found other means, for the sake of the gospel, and he will continue to do so. This is a genuine *boast* of Paul (verse 10). It is a boast that will be known throughout the Achaian province or all of southern Greece. Why should Paul boast in this matter? Certainly not because Paul does not love them! God knows that Paul loves them as children of God and as his spiritual offspring. Paul's statements make the Corinthian missionary intruders appear in a negative light.

And Paul has no intention of changing his activities and work. The other missionary workers apparently claimed the same status and work intentions of Paul and his fellow workers. Perhaps these other workers received material and financial support from those in Corinth. Paul serves only the gospel. He wholeheartedly supports and serves those in Corinth for the sake of the gospel. Unlike these other missionaries, Paul's intentions are genuine before God.

Now Paul identifies the character of these intruders. Paul uses two rather strong terms to describe them, *false* and *deceitful* (verse 13). These persons claim to be *apostles of Christ*. Paul is angry because these individuals dilute and distort the gospel. They are the most dangerous of persons and purposely disguise themselves as true apostles. Then Paul makes a statement about the nature of evil. As the serpent *deceived* Eve (verse 3), so anything contrary to God may attempt the disguise of a worshiper of God. Such a person may appear as godly, but in reality be only self-seeking and self-centered. Historically this has always been a problem in the area of religion, and not least of all in Christianity. Paul here makes an accusation against the intruding missionaries (verse 15). These individuals act as *servants* [NIV; NRSV= *ministers*] *of righteousness*. In the end, they will be judged in accordance with their deceitful deeds. In fact, they are hypocrites.

Now Paul turns to his own credentials as an apostle. Paul does not wish to appear *a fool* simply because he thinks he is wise (verse 16). In the worldly sense, such a superior attitude could prove a person to be very foolish indeed. Rather, Paul's foolishness is the opposite of worldly wisdom because Paul abases himself for the Corinthians (see verse 7). But if the Corinthians think he is foolish for having such an attitude toward themselves, let them momentarily accept his foolishness. This will allow him to boast just as the intruding missionaries have boasted about themselves. However, Paul wishes to make clear that his boasting is not done for the sake of Christ (verse 16). His boasting is sheer folly on his own part because of the situation at Corinth. That is to say, his boasting will not promote and bear witness to the Lord; it will only promote and bear witness to himself and to his own calling as an apostle. The things he is about to mention are worldly things, but he will indulge anyway, for a moment (verse 18).

With great irony, Paul explains why they should listen to his foolishness. Although they themselves are wise in the Lord, nevertheless they have patiently listened to the foolishness of boastful and false missionaries. Why should they not indulge Paul's boasting? After all, consider what these other persons have done (verse 20). These missionaries have dominated them, eaten their food, claimed authority over them, possibly even struck them on *the face* (although this is probably meant metaphorically). Paul admits that he did not practice such dominance over the Corinthian believers. This is to his *shame*! Perhaps Paul *should* have offered more leadership and dominance to the various congregations.

Paul now tells about himself and the intruding missionaries. They may speak Hebrew, but so does Paul. They claim citizenship with the people of God (*Israelites*), but so does Paul. Whatever they claim as Jewish (*descendants of Abraham*), Paul can claim the same. But do they serve Christ? Paul senses that he sounds like a madman, one who is boasting only in himself. He sounds like an egotist. But nevertheless, can they claim more than Paul? Then Paul lists a series of mishaps and experiences that must amaze the Corinthian believers. When these occurred during his long ministry is uncertain, and Paul offers no clue for identification. Paul's labors, imprisonments, beatings, and near-death sufferings attest to his genuine apostleship in the Lord.

Paul continues his boasting for several verses. A punishment used by the Jews (Deuteronomy 25:2-3) was forty lashes (or about forty; verse 24). Paul received this five times during his ministry. Rome punished its citizens (Acts 16:22) by beating with *rods* (verse 25). Paul was also stoned (a possible reference to Acts 14:19), *shipwrecked, adrift at sea* waiting to be rescued, often traveling on the road (verse 26), forced to cross treacherous bridgeless rivers, in danger of being mugged, hated by Jews and Gentiles, threatened in cities and *in the wilderness,* caught in storms at sea, and persecuted by *false brothers* (as in Corinth). What an astonishing list! All of this, plus general living conditions (verse 27), made Paul's life very uncomfortable indeed.

And these were merely external problems and difficulties. There were also internal pressures he had to cope with (verse 28). He was constantly concerned and anxious about the spiritual well-being of the churches he had founded around the Mediterranean world. Paul did not preach to them and abandon them. He continued to nurture, guide, and direct the house churches that he established. (Not to mention his *thorn . . . in the flesh,* (2 Corinthians 12:7-9.)

As a summary statement to all of Paul's suffering, he identifies his experiences as signs of weakness. If anyone is weak, Paul is certainly weak. His experiences during

1 AND 2 CORINTHIANS

the course of his ministry qualify him well for such status. In light of all this, Paul is angered. Why? Because after all of his sufferings, some in Corinth are made to fall by false apostles. In spite of Paul's long list of weaknesses and sufferings, some at Corinth have turned from the true gospel of Christ.

Nevertheless, Paul prefers to boast in the signs of his weakness. Ironically, he will not boast in his strengths, as the intruders at Corinth seem prone to do. Furthermore, by only boasting in his weaknesses, he does not distract the Corinthians from the gospel. In a very Jewish manner, he indicates his sincerity in all this by calling upon God as his witness. In concluding his thoughts, Paul introduces a new topic about his Damascus experience (verses 32-33). Perhaps, as some scholars have suggested, Paul is referring to a derogatory story that circulated around the Corinth house churches (see Acts 9:23-25). In any case, Paul relates this experience of his weakness, indicating that it was a rather humiliating event. Because the event tells how Paul was delivered by God from his enemies, Paul may have introduced it to indicate how God is strong in human weakness.

Paul continues to boast with the intention of emphasizing the gospel (12:10). His boasting is not for himself, but solely for the gospel and the risen Christ. Paul will boast with the hope that it will somehow direct the Corinthians anew to Christ.

Following rabbinic tradition, Paul speaks about *a man* (NIV; NRSV = *person*) when he means himself (verse 2). *In Christ* Paul can recall fourteen years ago, probably before the city of Corinth had heard of Christ, when he had a wonderful vision. Perhaps those in Corinth were quite keen to receive visions and revelations from God. Paul's vision was so dramatic and powerful that he could not determine whether he was in or out of his body. Only God, the originator of such an experience, knows for sure what Paul experienced. Paul refers to the *third heaven,* possibly an indication of perfection (three) and suggesting a peak spiritual experience. Paul then repeats his statements (verse 3), this time substituting *Paradise* for *third heaven*. The third heaven experience communicated a visual truth; the paradise experience revealed divine secrets in a verbal form. These secrets are so profound that they cannot be spoken to others. Paul has now spoken of things that must have greatly interested the Corinthians.

Speaking from the side of God, this person can boast. And Paul does boast, in Christ. But speaking out of his own human person, Paul refuses to *boast*. Paul will only emphasize his *weaknesses*. In this manner, Christ will remain the center of the gospel, and not Paul or his list of experiences. After all that has been said, Paul certainly could boast, and not be a fool in doing so, if he wished. But Paul insists that he must not become more important than Christ or the gospel. He and his experiences are not what make the gospel valid. He and his experiences are of no consequence in the presence of the risen Christ. In fact, Paul implies that all such experiences must be subjected to the completed work of reconciliation in Christ.

How does Paul cope with the temptations of putting great worth in these experiences? Paul was given a burden, a painful *thorn* in this flesh, *a messenger of Satan* to beat him and subject him to the truth of God in Christ. What was this thorn in Paul's flesh? Numerous explanations have been attempted, including epilepsy, malaria, and failing eyesight. In the end, no explanation is possible because Paul offers no clues other than this spiritual interpretation of a probable physical ailment. Paul understood his *thorn* as a reminder of his dependence upon God for reconciliation and new life. At first, Paul could not understand its meaning. He prayed to be relieved from this ailment. Then Paul takes this beautifully told personal account of a spiritual journey back to God. God's message about all this is clear enough. When a person is weak and throws himself or herself upon God in Christ, God's power makes that person strong. So Paul has been right all along with regard to boasting and weakness. He is *content*, knowing that his human frailty casts him eternally upon the power of God in Christ.

Paul concludes his defense. As an apostle called by God, Paul was greater than the *superlative* apostles because he pointed to Christ. The super apostles pointed to themselves. Yet, standing before God, Paul is nothing. He trusts only in Christ and gives no human value to his sufferings, accomplishments, calling, and leadership.

Paul has already accomplished *the signs of a true apostle* in Corinth (verse 12). He was patient, waiting upon the Lord to work in their midst. The result was tremendous (Acts 2:22). There were *signs, wonders,* and *mighty works* (NRSV; NIV = *miracles*). So what exactly was their complaint? The whole controversy seems to center on Paul's refusal to accept financial and material support from the Corinthian house churches (verse 13). This is the problem that keeps surfacing throughout this section (chapters 10–13). Apparently the Corinthians felt less favored because Paul did not *burden* them. Their pride was hurt. And their pride has opened the door to other distractions from the gospel of Christ. Paul concludes the section by apologizing for his actions, admitting that perhaps he was wrong in this matter.

§ § § § § § §

The Message of 2 Corinthians 10:1–12:13

In this section Paul focuses on the nature of his ministry and his authority as an apostle. In the face of apparent doubt and suspicion on the part of the Corinthians, Paul makes a personal appeal on behalf of the message he proclaims—the gospel of Jesus Christ.

§ § § § § § §

Introduction to These Verses

After all that has been said, Paul makes a final appeal
that the Corinthians keep themselves focused on Christ.
Paul is prepared to come yet again to visit them, for the
third time (verse 14; see also 13:1). Earlier in this epistle,
he had mentioned his hesitation in making a third visit,
almost certainly the painful visit (1:23 and 2:1). Paul is
now bold enough to visit them because he has had the
opportunity in letters to make his position clear.

An Appeal for Renewal in Christ (12:14–13:10)

Paul insists on certain conditions. First of all, he still
refuses to be a *burden* to the believers at Corinth. Even
though he has the right to claim support and financial
backing (see 11:7-11; 12:13), he will not do so on this
third visit. Then Paul states why his attitude remains
firm. Paul does not care one iota about gaining their
possessions and money. As a true apostle of the Lord he
simply wants them in Christ and does not want any gain
from them. He desires the most important gift of all, their
commitment to Christ and the gospel. The second
condition is that they respect him as a parent. Because he
is their only spiritual parent, it is his responsibility to
leave them well-endowed spiritually.

In the end, Paul will do anything for the spiritual
well-being of the Corinthian believers. He will give
all—spiritual and physical energy, time, money,

possessions—anything for their continued focus on Christ. And he will do this with joy! Paul argues using the biblical theme of God coming to humanity. As God has acted first toward humanity, so Paul seeks to act first and act favorably toward the Corinthians. But if he does act on their behalf first, can they ignore him? On the contrary, just as humanity is called to respond to God's reconciliation in Christ, they should respond to Paul's willing sacrifice and concern for their spiritual health.

But Paul cannot forget the criticism that must have been voiced against him, that he did not accept their support. He did *not burden* them by requiring financial and material support. Now he states the exact accusations that have been made against him. On the one hand, he let it be known that he did not ask or claim financial support for his own missionary efforts. On the other hand, he has requested money for the poor in Jerusalem. So he has been *crafty*, receiving money deceitfully under the name of a different cause. In this manner, he could claim that they never supported him personally.

But had Paul ever really defrauded them financially? Had any of his messengers taken advantage of the Corinthians? Paul had apparently sent at least one other courier besides Titus (verse 18; see 8:18, 22-24), although another brother had been sent by the churches (8:19; possibly the churches of Macedonia, the place from which Paul writes). Paul mentions only Titus and the brother he sent. Naturally the Corinthians were a little upset that the self-supporting Paul had requested money through different people for the poor in Jerusalem. But Paul argues that they must not distort the true intentions of him and his fellow workers.

Based on what Paul has been writing, the Corinthians probably think he has been simply *defending* himself (verse 19). Paul has not been focusing on himself, although what they read may appear as though he is preoccupied in this manner. No, Paul has been writing for one purpose. He has been attempting to relieve their suspicions of him and his helpers so that they can see Christ more clearly. They have been distracted. And Paul has been writing *in Christ* with the one purpose of recentering their attention.

Paul's concern is that he and the Corinthians will continue to misunderstand each other when he visits them (verse 20; 12:14; 13:1). Paul may find that they have been distracted from Christ—especially because of the foreign missionaries and the misunderstanding about money (11:7-11; 12:13). And because of their change, they may find that he is not the missionary leader they desire. Then Paul lists problems that would occur if rival apostles should get the upper hand. A divided church, especially a group of house churches, would certainly experience *quarreling, jealousy, anger,* and so forth. The situation is so serious that Paul may find no joy in his imminent visit. Paul will be humbled by God because he will discover that his ministry has not produced any believers or any fruit. On the contrary, he will discover in Corinth unrepentant sinners and habitual sins that will make him *mourn* (NRSV; NIV = *be grieved*) for their salvation.

With some anxiety, Paul now begins to organize his imminent pastoral visit (13:1). This is his third visit (see 12:14; visit one—Acts 18:1-18; during the second visit Paul was attacked by a rival apostle). Paul is clearly concerned, as he has just stated, that he will find serious problems among the house churches of Corinth. Holding to Jewish law (Deuteronomy 19:15), Paul says there must be witnesses to support accusations.

Those who are in error and who follow the false apostles should be warned. In his absence Paul wishes to make the situation clear as he apparently did during his second visit. He *will not spare* (NIV; NRSV = *be lenient*) them.

Where does Paul get his strength to face this situation? From the risen Lord Jesus Christ (verse 4). In this verse

Paul draws an analogy between himself and his fellow workers and Christ. Christ accepted our weakness and was *crucified*. But because of God's power, Christ sustained the suffering of our weakness and overcame death in the Resurrection. Paul must have in mind here his own weakness and suffering when he speaks of Christ's suffering. And he must also have in mind the power of God that is about to work in the midst of the Corinthian house churches when Paul arrives.

In the meantime, Paul encourages believers in Corinth to examine themselves before God. Do not be concerned about testing the false apostles or even Paul himself. If Christ lives in you, examine yourself in relation to Christ. For Paul, the ultimate test is Christ. And only the believer can honestly examine himself or herself in prayer to Christ. So Paul once again fans them in the direction of Christ in the hope that the resurrected Lord will prepare them for his third visit. In their Christ-centered self-examination, Paul's human hope is that they will discover that his presentation of the gospel at Corinth was not erroneous, a blunder, or a deviation from the truth of God (verse 6).

Paul and his fellow workers will support the Corinthians in prayer. Not only will Paul pray for their self-examination in Christ, but he will also pray that they will make no *wrong* decisions. On the one hand, Paul pushes them toward Christ, placing their spiritual future in the hands of the risen Lord. On the other hand, Paul makes it clear that he has no personal stake or concern for reputation before the Corinthians. In fact, he states that he is even willing to risk apostolic failure if they will only examine themselves prayerfully in Christ.

Now Paul reflects on the situation as it stands. Paul is pleased. When he and his workers are weak in Christ, the message of the gospel is allowed to be proclaimed without obstruction. In their weakness, they do not hinder the living, risen, and ascended Christ who is made known through the work of the Holy Spirit. When Paul is weak, the Corinthian believers are strong in Christ. When apostles do not obstruct the gospel, the hearers are stronger in the faith. So Paul sincerely prays that they will be restored once again and reestablished in Christ. Paul is saying all this for a clear purpose (verse 10). He wants to prepare them spiritually for his visit. He wants them to begin refocusing on Christ now. He wants to clear the path for a constructive and mature visit. He could use his authority later, but he senses that such a confrontation will be destructive rather than constructive.

§ § § § § § §

The Message of 2 Corinthians 12:14–13:10

The problems facing the Corinthian believers are the confusion over collections for the poor in Jerusalem and the teachings of false prophets. In these verses, Paul confronts both these problems. First of all, his purpose is to upbuild the Corinthian house churches. His understanding of upbuilding is to reestablish them on the foundation of Christ. There are no ulterior motives evident in Paul. His intended purpose is to firm up the Corinthians in Christ.

But how is this upbuilding to be done? There are no apostles or teachers available to help the Corinthians. Possibly there are false prophets or false apostles in their midst. The Corinthians are in need of sound teachings and spiritual help. Knowing that they are not capable of discovering God's truth in Christ by examining the Old Testament (1 Corinthians 1:26-31) and that they are generally immature in the faith (1 Corinthians 3:1-4), Paul tells them to examine themselves in Christ. He throws them back upon the living Christ in prayer. Paul has given the Corinthians an excellent preparation for his imminent visit.

§ § § § § § §

PART TWENTY 2 Corinthians 13:11-14

Introduction to These Verses

In his concluding comments, Paul makes one final request in the hope that things will be right when he visits.

A Final Appeal (13:11-13)

As he has done throughout the letter, Paul refers to those in Corinth as *brothers,* meaning fellow believers in Christ. He bids them farewell, and requests that they redirect themselves toward Christ and not some other person or teaching. In this manner, they would mend their ways or center themselves upon Christ. They should listen to Paul's counsel and seek to establish themselves and their churches on Christ. If they do this, they will *agree with one another* (NRSV; NIV = *be of one mind*)—they will have to agree because they will all be speaking and acting in Christ. Their foundation in Christ will keep them *in peace.* The *love and peace* of God through the power of the Holy Spirit will bind them together as a fellowship centered on Christ.

Paul instructs those in Corinth to *greet one another with a holy kiss* (verse 12). This frequent suggestion by Paul (Romans 16:16; 1 Corinthians 16:20) implies that the letter is being read in a congregational setting. Perhaps house churches would come together for special occasions when Paul's letters arrived, or perhaps the letters were read aloud during the morning worship service. The kiss became a common Christian greeting during the latter half of the first century (Acts 20:37; 1 Thessalonians 5:26; 1 Peter 5:14). It was considered holy or a kiss of peace because it was exchanged in the name of God, representing God's love for all humanity expressed in Christ. To kiss a fellow believer was to acknowledge a common savior and a common faith. In the spirit of the holy kiss, Paul tells the Corinthians that all the *saints* or believers with whom Paul is acquainted extend their warm greetings in Christ (verse 13).

A Blessing of Grace (13:14)

The letter ends as it began, with a general blessing. This was a very common Jewish practice that Paul retained from his Jewish tradition. But Paul's benediction here is unique and noteworthy for several reasons. First of all, it is the most lengthy benediction that has survived the ages. Second, Paul mentions all three names of the Godhead—*Christ, God,* and the *Holy Spirit* (even though he does not use the term *trinity,* a word not found in the Scriptures). During the mid-fifties of the first century A.D., the later trinitarian controversies (second and third centuries) were not evident. Yet here we find Paul giving a clear early church formula for the Godhead.

Third, Paul indicates the role or work of each person in the Godhead. *Grace* is the divine movement toward humanity expressed in Jesus the Christ. In Christ, humanity hears God's resounding *Yes! I love you!* (1:19-20). God's agape love (1 Corinthians 13) is what sends the word of Christ, the Son of the Father. God freely and first chose to have fellowship with humanity. It is God's love that now and forever holds humanity in true existence—in right relationship to God. That which binds together God the Father and God the Son is God the Holy Spirit. This same Holy Spirit unites all the believers and all the house churches of Corinth together in eternal fellowship.

§ § § § § § §

The Message of 2 Corinthians 13:11-14

Paul's final words place all the emphasis on God. Throughout the letter, Paul centers all his attention on Christ. Even in his "boastful" section (chapters 11–12), everything is said for the single purpose of directing the Corinthian believers to God. Now here in his final statement (and in good Jewish tradition), Paul ends where he began: with God. His thanksgiving is always from God to humanity. Yet he does not fail to deal with the problems and stresses and strains of the Corinthians. But he does so by beginning with God, subjecting their difficulties to God's word spoken in Christ, and ending with God. This benediction is a fitting summary to his Corinthian epistles. It recognizes that God has reconciled humanity in Christ once and forever. Individuals are now called to believe and respond to God's love through Christ and in the Holy Spirit.

§ § § § § § §

Glossary of Terms

Achaia: The general name for the lower or southern portion of the Greek peninsula. The city of Corinth was the capital of this Roman province.

Agape: This is the New Testament Greek word for love. For Christians, especially for Paul, it came to mean the unmerited self-giving love of God toward humanity.

Apollos: A Jewish Christian from Alexandria in Egypt. He was an eloquent speaker and was instructed in the Christian faith by Aquila and Prisca.

Apostle: Paul refers to himself as an *apostle*, a term literally meaning *one who is sent forth*. An early understanding of *apostle* was that of one who was an eyewitness of Jesus.

Cephas: In the Aramaic language (the language Jesus spoke), this term means *rock*. In the Gospels it is equal to the Greek name *Peter*.

Circumcision: A Jewish ritual that removes the foreskin from the penis. It was a rather common practice by many cultures of the ancient Near East. In Jewish ritual, the ceremony was almost always performed on the eighth day after birth. Theologically, it is understood as a sign of God's covenant with Israel. Later, during the time of Jesus and Paul, it was understood as the ritual that brought a child under the law of Moses and made him responsible for keeping the law.

Cosmology: This term refers to an understanding of the order and arrangement of the universe. The Greek term *kosmos* means *world* or *universe*; the term *logos* means a discourse about something.

Dispersion (Diaspora): The emigration of Jews from Palestine. It was during the Hellenistic period (332 B.C.–A.D. 63) that Jews immigrated to the city of Corinth.

Dispensation: This is actually a Latin term meaning to administer something. It is used to translate the Greek term for *ministry* in 2 Corinthians 3:7-8.

Faith: This term means to focus all one's attention on God. In the New Testament, especially in the writings of Paul, faith is understood as a gift from God. Like hope and love, Paul understands faith's content as based only in God's activity through Christ and in the Holy Spirit.

Fornication: This term refers to any type of sexual misconduct, including adultery, rape, sodomy, seduction, incest, prostitution, homosexual activity, and so forth. Adultery was considered the most serious type of fornication, because marriage symbolized the covenant relationship between God and Israel.

Gnosticism: A term used to describe a number of religious movements during the New Testament period and for several centuries thereafter. The term comes from a Greek word, *gnosis*, meaning *knowledge* or *wisdom*. This religious belief taught that salvation from the material world could be gained by receiving a special spiritual knowledge or wisdom. Because Gnostic groups were evident in the city of Corinth, it has been argued that Paul was battling serious Gnostic influences.

Immorality: As opposed to *amoral* (having no morals) and *morality* (usually referring to right or accepted standards), immorality refers to questionable or inadequate moral behavior. The word *moral* refers to conduct, action, or sometimes character.

Justified, justification: This term means to be put right with something, such as a law. In the New Testament, it refers to humanity being put right with God's law of love.

Kosher: This is a transliteration of a Hebrew word meaning *pure* or *clean*. The term is used to describe foods

that have been prepared in the proper manner. Right preparation expresses thanksgiving and honor to God.
Pagans: This Latin term originally referred to rustic, rural, or country folk. Tertullian (about A.D. 160–215) used it to describe non-Christians. In 1 Corinthians 6:1, Paul refers to the courts of the *unrighteous.* These unbelievers eventually became known as *pagans.*
Pentateuch (Torah): Torah is a Hebrew word meaning *law.* *Pentateuch* is a Greek word meaning *five.* The first five books of the Old Testament were considered God's essential law for the Hebrews.
Rabbi (Rabboni): The Hebrew word literally means *my great one* and refers to one called to God's service. Eventually, when the Scriptures became very important for Israel, the term came to mean *teacher* or one who interprets God's law.
Sacrament: Originally, this term had secular meanings in the Roman world. For example, it was used to describe a soldier's oath, and as a designation for a deposit of money in the law courts. When the Bible was translated from Greek into Latin, the Greek word *mysterios* (mystery) was translated with the term *sacramentum* (sacrament). Thus the "mysteries" of the Christian faith became "sacraments" in Western Christianity.
Saints: This term refers to persons who are special because of their relationship with God. Paul uses this term to refer to church members.
Sanctification: This refers to making something holy (places, persons, and so forth). When, for example, a person is kept aside for God's service, he or she is being sanctified. The term is ongoing and is not meant—as *saint*—to be understood in a static sense.
Satan: The Hebrew word means *adversary.* Satan and his helpers are understood in the Scriptures as the powers of evil in the world. The helpers of Satan, called demons, devils, accusers, evil ones, and so forth, cause all types of illnesses, catastrophies, and disasters.

Guide to Pronunciation

Abba: AB-bah
Achaia: Ah-KAY-ah
Agape: Ah-GAH-pay
Apollos: Ah-PAH-lus
Apostasy: Ah-PAHS-tah-see
Aquila: Ah-KWILL-ah
Aretas: AH-reh-tas
Cephas: SEE-fus
Chloe: KLOH-wee
Crispus: KRIS-pus
Damascus: Dah-MASS-kus
Ephesus: EH-feh-sus
Fortunatus: For-too-NAH-tus
Gaius: GAY-us
Galatia: Gah-LAY-shuh
Gnosticism: NAHS-tih-sih-zum
Macedonia: Mass-eh-DOH-nee-ah
Paschal: PASS-kul
Pentateuch: PEN-tah-tuke
Philippi: FILL-ih-pigh
Philippians: Fih-LIP-ee-ans
Silvanus: Sil-VAN-us
Sosthenes: SAHS-thuh-neez
Stephanas: STEH-fah-nus
Troas: TROH-ahs

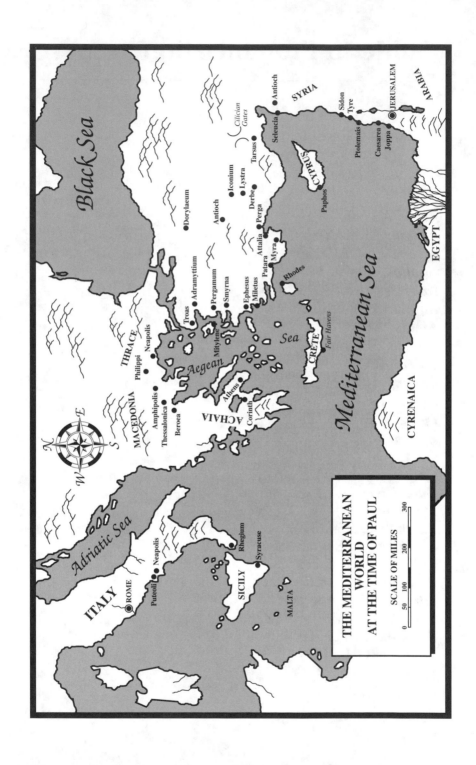

Black Sea

Doryleaum

Cilician
Gates

SYRIA

Antioch

Seleucia
Sidon
Tyre

JERUSALEM

ARABIA

Antioch

Iconium
Lystra
Derbe
Perga

CYPRUS

Ptolemais
Caesarea
Joppa

Tarsus

Paphos

Attalia
Myra
Patara
Rhodes

EGYPT

THRACE

Adramyttium
Pergamum
Smyrna
Ephesus
Miletus

Troas

Mitylene

Neapolis

Aegean
Sea

Fair Havens

CRETE

Mediterranean Sea

Philippi

Athens

MACEDONIA

Amphipolis

Corinth

ACHAIA

CYRENAICA

Thessalonica
Beroea

N
E
W
S

Adriatic Sea

Rhegium
Syracuse

Neapolis

SICILY

MALTA

ITALY

Puteoli

ROME

THE MEDITERRANEAN
WORLD
AT THE TIME OF PAUL

SCALE OF MILES

0 50 100   200   300